Emblem used on the joint stock built for the electric working of the Hammersmith & City Railway. The elaborate scroll-work made it a distinctive device, but few people thought it exactly a masterpiece of design. It has, however, a 'period' flavour which, at this distance, is not without interest

Elaborate new device introduced by the Metropolitan Railway shortly after the original electrification of 1905. The arms are the City of London (top left), pre-1910 form of the County of Middlesex (top right), County of Buckingham (the Swan, lower left), and County of Hertford (the Hart, lower right). The background of crimson and ermine mantling is surmounted by a clenched fist radiating electrical energy

Steam to Silver

An illustrated history of
London Transport railway
surface rolling stock

J. Graeme Bruce

B.Sc.(Eng.)., F.I.E.E., F.I.Mech.E., M.Inst.T.

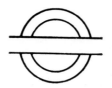

London Transport
55 Broadway Westminster
S.W.1

Cover: CIRCLE LINE ROLLING STOCK

Drawing of original Metropolitan 'A' class steam engine used on the
Inner Circle   (Top Left)

Drawing of London Transport's latest C69 Circle Line rolling stock

Introduction

by R. M. Robbins
Member, London Transport Executive

Railway rolling stock has a history of development arising for two main reasons: advancement of technique which enables existing and known requirements to be met more adequately and reliably as knowledge of materials is improved and new types of equipment are devised; and—what often seems to progress even faster— changing requirements on the part of operators and passengers which constantly keep the rolling stock engineers on the search for solutions to new or altered problems.

The requirements of an urban underground railway system are severe: in function, the rolling stock must perform its duty with the utmost efficiency, carrying large numbers of passengers securely and at brief intervals enabling them to get in and out with great speed; in performance, good acceleration and braking are paramount; in reliability, maintenance must be easily carried out, and as little of it as possible; financially, it must be economical in first cost, in maintenance, and in power consumption.

Mr. Bruce has set down here, with as much clarity as the nature of the subject allows, the story of the development of the rolling stock constructed for the 'surface' (or sub-surface) lines of London's underground railway system. Starting from the original steam-hauled carriages of the Metropolitan and Metropolitan District Railways (which, it must be confessed, were not very enterprising in their activity in this field) through the early, exciting, and experimental days of their electrification in the first decade of the twentieth century to the complex sequence of construction and shuffling which followed the amalgamation of the two railways under the London Passenger Transport Board in 1933, and so to the present time. If any one feature more than another stands out from his account, it is the necessity, so skilfully met by successive generations of engineers, to compromise what they would like to do with the imperious demands of the operators— themselves attempting to cope with surges of passenger traffic, restricted stations, and rigid patterns of operation imposed by tunnel conditions and track layouts. That will remain the rolling stock engineer's most taxing task.

Mr. Bruce enables his readers to judge how far the conditions of effective and efficient operation have been met, by setting down this tale of the successes—in a few cases, the less than complete successes—that the designers have achieved.

Preface

The history of the Surface Rolling Stock of London Transport is more complicated and much less of a continuous story than that of the deep level Tube Rolling Stock, covered in the companion volume 'Tube Trains Under London'. The Metropolitan Railway and the District Railway had different rolling stock policies which, after the formation of London Transport, had to be consolidated, but the tradition of the two railways which eventually became one in 1933 died hard. This story of the rolling stock of these two railways and subsequent developments, was impossible to write in a condensed and continuous form without also including a considerable amount of information on operating policy and track arrangements because these matters have materially affected the trains used.

Car numbers have been used sparingly, being given only where their inclusion adds directly to the understanding of the text. Where two sets of numbers are given those shown in brackets provide the number allocated by London Transport after 1933. The term 'coach' is used to describe any compartment type vehicle with swing doors, all other vehicles of the open saloon type are called 'cars' in accordance with the practice adopted by London Transport and to some extent by the Metropolitan Railway previously.

Each section deals as far as possible with a particular subject from beginning to end and so covers a wide span of years. There is some overlapping and repetition of information to make each section a complete story.

The information contained in these pages spans over 100 years of development and has in some cases been difficult to collect but I am grateful to a great many of my colleagues, both serving and retired, who are too numerous to mention by name, for the information they have wittingly or unwittingly provided for this book during the past few years. However, I must specially mention Mr. H. Clarke and Mr. John Day who have worked particularly hard at proof reading and date checking. Mr. Charles E. Lee has also been helpful with his specialist knowledge of railway history. The information on the C69 stock is provided by kind permission of Mr. G. S. Bingham, London Transport's Chief Mechanical Engineer (Design and Development), who has been responsible for its introduction into service.

I must also render my grateful thanks to Mr. K. R. Benest for his painstaking researches into the history of the Metropolitan Railway which have enabled some of the more obscure information to be clarified. In addition my correspondence and discussions with Mr. B. J. Prigmore, another rolling stock student, have impressed me with the need to double check any information culled from an historical article or photograph caption. Even then I am afraid there will be some inaccuracies in this book; those of fact must be laid at my door.

J.G.B.

**The cover of this book was designed
by William Fenton, A.R.C.A.**

The companion volume Tube Trains under London by J. Graeme Bruce is available, price 12/6d., from London Transport Enquiry Offices at Piccadilly Circus, Oxford Circus, King's Cross, Euston, Victoria, and St. James's Park Underground stations. Or, post free, from the Publicity Officer, London Transport, 280 Old Marylebone Road, London, N.W.1.

Contents and list of illustrations

Note: The sketch maps in this book are outline only, and do not show sidings and goods lines

SOME TECHNICAL ABBREVIATIONS

M   Motor Car/Coach.

3M   Third Class Motor Car/Coach.

DM   Double-Equipped Motor Car/Coach.

SM   Single-Equipped Motor Car/Coach.

NDM   Non-driving Motor Car.

CT   Control Trailer Car/Coach.

T   Trailer Car/Coach.

3T   Third Class Trailer Car/Coach.

1/3T   Composite First and Third Class Trailer Car/Coach.

1T   First Class Trailer Car/Coach.

2T   Second Class Trailer Car/Coach.

B2T   Second Class Brake Van.

B3T   Third Class Brake Van.

BWE   British Westinghouse Electric & Manufacturing Co.

BTH   British Thomson-Houston Co.

GEC   General Electric Co.

METRO   Metropolitan-Cammell Ltd. or its predecessors.

AEI   Associated Electrical Industries Ltd.

LNWR   London & North Western Railway.

LBSC   London, Brighton & South Coast Railway.

SER   South Eastern Railway.

LSWR   London & South Western Railway.

LMS   London Midland & Scottish Railway.

H & C   Hammersmith & City Railway.

GWR   Great Western Railway.

Cycles   Cycles per second.

1 | The beginning

The Circle Line, still known by many as the Inner Circle, is the oldest of London's Underground lines. It was always known as the Inner Circle until recent times, because for many years there were also a Middle Circle and Outer Circle. Most of the traces of these, however, have now been lost.

It all began over 100 years ago when the first section of the Metropolitan Railway was opened from Bishop's Road (Paddington) to Farringdon Street on 10 January 1863. Construction of the line started properly in 1860 with the financial support of the Great Western Railway and the Corporation of the City of London, inspired by its Solicitor, Charles Pearson, who was the driving force during the planning stages. The scheme was also backed by the Great Northern Railway which wanted to use the new line to gain access to the City.

The line was built on the 'cut and cover' principle just below the street level and, because the motive power to be used was steam, provision was made for gratings and open-ings to clear the tunnels of fumes. The tracks were laid with dual gauge using three rails so that trains of both standard gauge (4 ft. 8½ in.) and the Great Western broad gauge (7 ft. 0¼ in.) could use the tunnels. The Metropolitan Railway made an end-on junction at Bishop's Road with the Great Western Railway.

The Circle Line since then has seen, on some sections of the track at least, all the surface rolling stock developed by London Transport and its predecessors, the Metropolitan Railway and the Metropolitan District Railway (known and referred to subsequently as the District Railway) as well as some of the London suburban rolling stock of several main line railways.

The latest rolling stock, designated 'C69' stock (C for Circle, 69 for the year of its actual birth), is now going into service on the Hammersmith & City and Circle Lines, completing the story of London Transport's surface rolling stock for the time being.

Following the opening of the first section of the Metropolitan, an eastward extension to Moorgate was brought into service on 23 December 1865. This remained the eastern terminus of the line until Bishopsgate (now Liverpool Street) was reached some 10 years later. This point was reached in two stages. Initially tracks were laid into the Liverpool Street terminal of the Great Eastern Railway and a service was operated from there beginning 1 February 1875. The Metropolitan

1 *Broad gauge Great Western train at Praed Street Junction*

station, named Bishopsgate until 1909, was not ready until 12 July 1875. A connection was opened with the Great Northern Railway at King's Cross in October 1863. Soon after the completion of the line to Moorgate it was decided to quadruple the tracks between King's Cross and Moorgate. These additional tracks known as the 'City Widened Lines' are still in use today but not for electric trains. The section of the Widened Lines between Farringdon and Aldersgate was brought into use on 1 March 1866, that between Aldersgate and Moorgate on 1 July 1866, and both were joined up with the main line tracks near King's Cross and St. Pancras on 17 February 1868. This enabled the Midland Railway to open a service to [2] Moorgate Street on 13 July 1868, some months before its own terminus at St. Pancras was brought into use.

While all this was going on at the eastern end of the new line, a separate company built a branch railway at the western end to Hammersmith. This was opened on 13 June 1864, and is now the western terminus of the Hammersmith & City Line of London Transport. A branch to Kensington (Addison Road) left the Hammersmith line near Latimer Road station and connected with the West London Railway, providing a valuable link with the railways of South London. This spur (now removed) was, however, important in the story because it provided eventually the means of running a Middle Circle service.

The Metropolitan Railway was also extending its line to the west by branching off after Edgware Road station to South Kensington. This line was opened to Gloucester Road on 1 October 1868, and to South Kensington 12 weeks later, to make a junction with the new railway—the District Railway—which was opened from South Kensington to Westminster Bridge station on 24 December 1868, and then to Blackfriars on 30 May 1870. The trains were worked by the Metropolitan until 3 July 1871, when the District acquired its own rolling stock.

The District constructed its own tracks from South Kensington to Gloucester Road on the south side of the Metropolitan tracks and then branched away to West Brompton. A shuttle service from Gloucester Road to West Brompton was operated by the Metropolitan on behalf of the District from 12 April 1869. In addition, at about the same time, the District constructed a line in the shape of a U-bend from the Kensington High Street junction with the Metropolitan, through Earl's Court, to the West London Railway at Kensington (Addison Road), in this way joining the West Brompton line for a short distance. The first regular service between Kensington High Street and Cromwell Road junction began on 3 July

2 *An Inner Circle train approaching Aldgate, about 1900*

1871; and from Earl's Court to Kensington (Addison Road) on 1 February, 1872.

This connection to Addison Road provided the means of working both the Middle and the Outer Circle services. The District was extended eastwards on 3 July 1871 to

the East London Railway became possible. The station called Tower of London (on the site of the present Tower Hill) was closed on 13 October 1884, being replaced by

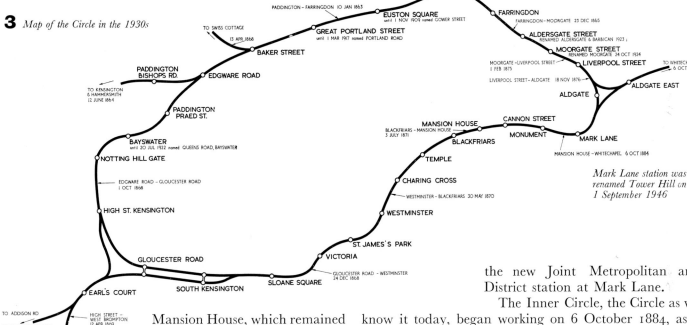

3 *Map of the Circle in the 1930s*

KING'S CROSS

PADDINGTON — FARRINGDON 10 JAN 1863

EUSTON SQUARE
until 1 NOV 1909 named GOWER STREET

FARRINGDON
FARRINGDON — MOORGATE 23 DEC 1865

TO SWISS COTTAGE
13 APR 1868

GREAT PORTLAND STREET
until 1 MAR 1917 named PORTLAND ROAD

ALDERSGATE STREET
RENAMED ALDERSGATE & BARBICAN 1923 ;

MOORGATE STREET
RENAMED MOORGATE 24 OCT 1924

BAKER STREET

MOORGATE — LIVERPOOL STREET
1 FEB 1875

LIVERPOOL STREET

TO WHITECHAPEL
6 OCT 1884

PADDINGTON BISHOPS RD.

EDGWARE ROAD

LIVERPOOL STREET — ALDGATE 18 NOV 1876

ALDGATE EAST

TO KENSINGTON & HAMMERSMITH 12 JUNE 1864

PADDINGTON PRAED ST.

ALDGATE

MANSION HOUSE

CANNON STREET

BAYSWATER
until 20 JUL 1922 named QUEENS ROAD, BAYSWATER

BLACKFRIARS — MANSION HOUSE
3 JULY 1871

MONUMENT

MARK LANE

NOTTING HILL GATE

BLACKFRIARS

MANSION HOUSE — WHITECHAPEL 6 OCT 1884

EDGWARE ROAD — GLOUCESTER ROAD
1 OCT 1868

TEMPLE

Mark Lane station was renamed Tower Hill on 1 September 1946

HIGH ST. KENSINGTON

CHARING CROSS

WESTMINSTER — BLACKFRIARS 30 MAY 1870

WESTMINSTER

ST. JAMES'S PARK

GLOUCESTER ROAD

VICTORIA

EARL'S COURT

SOUTH KENSINGTON

SLOANE SQUARE

GLOUCESTER ROAD — WESTMINSTER
24 DEC 1868

TO ADDISON RD

HIGH STREET — WEST BROMPTON
12 APR 1869

TO HAMMERSMITH 1874

WEST BROMPTON

TO PUTNEY BRIDGE AND WIMBLEDON

the new Joint Metropolitan and District station at Mark Lane.

The Inner Circle, the Circle as we know it today, began working on 6 October 1884, as a joint service of both the Metropolitan and District Railways. The trains which ran in a clockwise direction—that is on the outer rail of the circle—were provided by the Metropolitan, while those on the inner rail, working anti-clockwise round the circle, were provided by the District. From time to time some Metropolitan trains had to work on the anti-clockwise service, to equate the mileage, as by far the greater proportion of the trackage of the Circle was owned by the Metropolitan. Before the completion

Mansion House, which remained the eastern terminus until 6 October 1884, when the Metropolitan and the District Joint Line was built joining Mansion House with Aldgate and Whitechapel. The Metropolitan reached the Aldgate terminus on 18 November 1876, and extended its line to Tower of London Station on 25 September 1882, but the triangular junction with the District was not completed until 1884 when through running to

[3

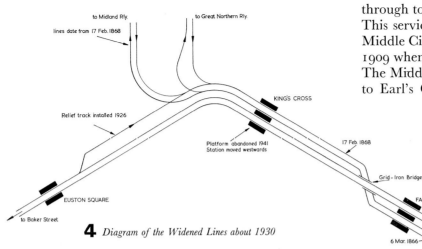

to Midland Rly.

to Great Northern Rly.

lines date from 17 Feb. 1868

KING'S CROSS

Relief track installed 1926

Platform abandoned 1941
Station moved westwards

17 Feb. 1868

Grid - Iron Bridge

EUSTON SQUARE

FARRINGDON

to Baker Street

ALDERSGATE

4 *Diagram of the Widened Lines about 1930*

6 Mar. 1866

1 July 1866

MOORGATE

to Holborn H.L.
Southern Railway

to Liverpool Street

through to the District Railway to reach Mansion House. This service, also a horseshoe in form, was known as the Middle Circle. The Outer Circle survived until 1 January 1909 when the service ceased to work east of Earl's Court. The Middle Circle service on the other hand was cut back to Earl's Court on 30 June 1900, ceasing altogether on 31 January 1905. A remnant of this service survived under electrification as a shuttle connection from H & C stations to Addison

of the Circle, however, the train service from Moorgate, and later Aldgate, to Mansion House was known as the Inner Circle. On 1 February 1872 the London & North Western Railway began working a train service from Broad Street by way of the North London line and the West London Railway to Earl's Court and Mansion House. This was, in fact, a variant of a service which had worked into Victoria L.B.S.C. station by much of the same route. This service, worked throughout at this time with LNWR locomotives and rolling stock, was known as the Outer Circle, although this too was horseshoe-shaped, and not a complete circle. On 1 August of the same year the Great Western Railway began working standard gauge trains between Moorgate on the Metropolitan by way of the Hammersmith & City Line to Addison Road and

Road, but has now disappeared. Only the Inner Circle remains, so that today the service is known simply as the Circle Line.

A short-lived Midland Railway service between St. Pancras and Earl's Court by way of Cricklewood, Acton, and Hammersmith, a kind of 'Outer' Outer Circle, was operated from 1 May 1878 to 30 September 1880 after the District train service had been extended to Richmond.

2 | The original Underground trains

When the service on the Underground first began, the rolling stock was provided by the Great Western Railway which owned a shareholding in the company. The locomotives and carriages were of broad gauge. By July 1863, relations between the Great Western Railway and the Metropolitan had deteriorated to such an extent that the Great Western decided to withdraw its rolling stock and it ceased maintaining the service on the evening of 10 August. The Great Northern Railway then provided both the locomotives and many of the carriages until the Metropolitan Railway could obtain rolling stock of its own. It was not until July 1864 that sufficient vehicles were available for full operation by the Metropolitan on its own account.

The original order for 18 steam locomotives was placed with Beyer, Peacock & Co. of Gorton, Manchester. These original locomotives were the famous 'A' class, which was [5]

5 *One of the original 'A' class Metropolitan Railway locomotives outside Edgware Road engine sheds*

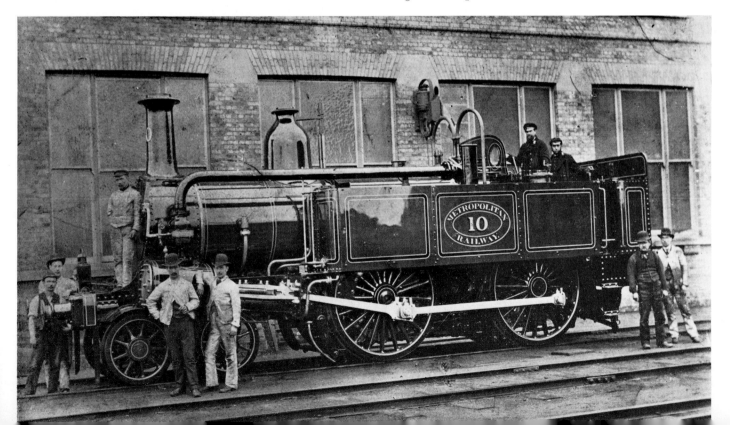

the basic design for practically all the locomotives used on the Underground operations until electrification. Forty-four of the 'A' class were built between 1864 and 1870 followed up to 1885 by a further 22 of the improved 'B' type. The District Railway obtained 54 similar locomotives between 1871 and 1886. This locomotive type, a 4–4–0 type tank engine can, therefore, be considered the pioneer motive power on London's Underground.

As originally built they did not have cabs, just a spectacle plate or weather board for the protection of the driver. The District locomotives could, in later years, be distinguished from the Metropolitan by the fact that this weather board was not flat, being curved at the top over the footplate.

The original livery of both railways was similar, at least when dirty. The Metropolitan livery was described as dark green and the District dull green. The Metropolitan changed the livery to chocolate brown, described by some authorities as dark red, about 1885. The original

18 locomotives were named, but subsequent locomotives were distinguished at first only by a brass number carried on the front of the chimney. When the colour was changed the numbers were painted on the side tanks.

All the original Metropolitan locomotives were designed for 'left hand' cab driving position, because of the need for the driver to observe thoroughly the station duties and yet make a quick start away. Most stations on the Circle had conventional platforms. Wrong side positioning for the driver, therefore, occurred only at the terminals, or when running bunker first.

The engines weighed about 46½ tons in running order with 1,000 gallons of water in the side tanks. The coupled wheels were 5 ft. 9 in. in diameter driven by two 17-inch cylinders, with a stroke of 24 inches inclined at 1 in 9. The original boiler pressure was 120 lbs. per sq. in. but on the later locomotives this was raised to 160 lbs. per sq. in. Despite condensing arrangements, stations such as Temple and Portland Road (now Great Portland Street) were always full of thick sulphurous fumes. When the Circle service was complete the Metropolitan loco-

6 *A composite First and Second Class eight-wheeled coach, the original Metropolitan-type rolling stock*

motives took on coal and water at Edgware Road, the District locomotives at Kensington High Street.

The order for the original carriage stock was also placed in Manchester, with the Ashbury Railway Carriage & Iron Co. The first vehicles were similar in design to the Great Western Railway's but standard gauge instead of broad gauge. As they were narrower, they had relatively high roofs to accommodate the gas bags provided for lighting. The Great Western had, in fact, pioneered the introduction of coal gas lighting for the stock to be used on the Underground and the Metropolitan continued with this arrangement. The gas at this time was not compressed but carried in inflatable weighted bags on the carriage roofs. The 39 ft. 6 in. body, constructed mainly of teak, was built on an angle-iron frame which was about 6 inches shorter than the body. There were three different body arrangements in a standard length: First Class with six compartments, Second and Third Class with eight compartments, and composite with seven compartments containing three First Class compartments in the middle of the coach. The doors of the compartments originally had square tops. It was in 1867 that the traditional Metropolitan-type rounded-top door, reducing the liability to damage in the tunnels, was introduced.

The original vehicles were 42 feet long over buffers and were carried on four axles grouped in pairs but not provided with bogies. Flexibility at curves was provided by a translation movement of the radial axlebox attached to the mainframes by means of links hung from the ends of the springs at angles of about 30 degrees. The outer wheels of each pair were over 6 feet from the ends of the coach so that the vehicle, apart from the translation movement, was virtually rigid wheelbased. This arrangement varied on the different batches of stock and was finally modified on the introduction of the automatic

vacuum brake. When the vehicles were introduced the only brake fitted was Newall's handbrake in the guard's compartment which applied wooden brake blocks to four wheels of that coach.

The Wilkins and Clark chain brake which was later improved by Francis Webb, the famous Locomotive Engineer of the London & North Western Railway, was adopted in 1869. This was a form of continuous brake, in that a cord passing over the roofs of the carriage released weights which then operated the handbrake lever in the guard's compartment provided on each car. This brake, although effective, was very jerky and resulted in a number of serious injuries to passengers. In 1875 Smith's simple vacuum brake was adopted, to be converted later to the automatic vacuum. The Westinghouse air brake was not introduced on the Metropolitan until electric traction.

These vehicles were long in comparison with most railway passenger rolling stock of the time which was normally based on the rigid 4-wheeled frame. Trains of five of these carriages carried a large complement of passengers.

In 1870 the Metropolitan began acquiring from the Oldbury Carriage Co. some more carriages which were 4-wheeled, coupled in pairs. Each pair was close coupled, the pair measuring 43 ft. 8 in. in length—almost equivalent to the earlier 8-wheeled vehicles. Each body of the coupled pairs was 20 feet long and contained either three First Class compartments or four Second or Third Class compartments. The wheels were 42 inches in diameter, the springing being provided by 5 ft. long carriage-type springs mounted on top of the axleboxes. A combined central buffer and coupling provided the semi-permanent connection between the two-car sets but the outer ends were fitted with Sterne's patent buffing gear which had a pneumatic action. The width over the mouldings was 8 ft. 3 in.; inside the compartments the maximum height was 7 ft. 1 in.

The First Class compartments seated four passengers aside with arm rests. The Third Class compartments with wooden bench seats were only 4 ft. 10 in. between partitions. Partitions between First Class compartments were of full height but in the lower-class compartments only waist-height partitions were provided. One distinguishing feature of this stock, however, was the provision of small narrow windows (toplights) above the normal side windows (the quarter lights) of the compartments. This feature had also been provided in the 8-wheeled stock.

Coal gas lighting was provided with two lamps in the First Class compartments but only one in each compartment of the other two classes staggered across the vehicle.

The lamps were fed through iron pipes from the rubber gas bags, each bag being designed to fold up as the gas was used up. They were provided with an indicator which showed E for Empty or F for Full. Gas holders were provided at certain strategic points to replenish the gas bags of the carriages, but it was not until the Julius Pintsch system was adopted that the gas was provided in containers under pressure.

At first both the Metropolitan and the District did not provide smoking compartments as they had been specifically exempted from the Railway Regulation Act 1868 which required all railways to provide smoking accommodation. However, to meet public demand, and because the rolling stock of main-line railways which ran over the Metropolitan made provision for smokers, both the Metropolitan and the District introduced Smoking carriages on 1 September 1874.

[8]

7 *A Metropolitan train composed of five 8-wheeled coaches and one 4-wheeled coach*

3 | District Steam Stock

From 3 July 1871, the District Railway began working the services with their own rolling stock. The District Railway at this time ran from Mansion House in the east through South Kensington, where a junction with the Metropolitan Railway was made (with parallel tracks through Gloucester Road). The line then turned south to Earl's Court to terminate at West Brompton in the west. The first Earl's Court station was opened on 31 October 1871, amidst market gardens. The extension to Hammersmith was not opened to traffic until 9 September 1874, the year smoking compartments were first provided on both the District and the Metropolitan.

Between 1871 and 1886 the District purchased 54 Beyer, Peacock locomotives which were only different in detail from those supplied to the Metropolitan. The Metropolitan went on to build other types of locomotives as the need arose. The District, however, remained [9]

8 *District Railway engine No. 25 as originally built by Beyer, Peacock*

9 *District Railway engine No. 33 and 3-coach train of 4-wheeled stock. The locomotive is in its modified condition*

faithful to this original locomotive class for all the passenger working until electrification. The earlier locomotives had a leading Bissell radial swivelling 4-wheeled truck, but the later deliveries had Adams bogies and the earlier locomotives were converted. There were a number of differences between the earlier and later locomotives which could be easily distinguished by the expert. For example, the first 36 locomotives had brass dome covers with integral safety valves; later locomotives had safety valves over the fireboxes. Some of the earlier locomotives were modified to conform to this arrangement. The weather plate was bent back to give some protection to the crew. The back plate of the coal bunker was also raised over 1 foot to provide protection when running bunker first which was a regular practice, as turntables were not provided. The average coal consumption of these locomotives was 30 lbs. a mile.

All 54 of the locomotives of the District Railway were still in service in 1905 when electrification took place.

The District Railway constructed a maintenance yard and depot at Lillie Bridge, the access being made west of Earl's Court. It was completed by the summer of 1872.

The original trains on the District Railway were composed of eight 4-wheeled carriages. The make-up of these trains consisted of two First Class, two Second Class, and four Third Class, the classes being distinguished by large numbers painted on the compartment doors. There were four compartments in First Class coaches and five in the others. Each compartment was designed to seat five a side, even the First Class. Apart from the additional width in the First Class, the class distinction was achieved by varying the quality of the upholstery.

A short connecting line was built from Hammersmith to a point known as Studland Road junction which enabled the District Railway to gain access to the Kensington to Richmond line of the London & South Western Railway. Running powers were given to the District Railway and the service to Richmond commenced on 1 June 1877.

The District Railway then began constructing an extension on this line from Turnham Green to Ealing Broadway, which was opened on 1 July 1879. Powers were sought for an extension to Uxbridge but these were opposed by the Great Western Railway. However, as some sort of compensation, a connection with the Great Western was constructed at Ealing Broadway so that on 1 March 1883, a through service of District trains was inaugurated to Windsor. Twenty-two through trains were worked on weekdays, but the traffic did not reach expectations and the service was withdrawn on 30 September 1885.

At Mill Hill Park (now Acton Town) the Hounslow & Metropolitan Railway, at first a separate undertaking but worked by the District, branched southwards to Hounslow Town, the service being opened on 1 May 1883. Just over a year later, on 21 July 1884, the single line to Hounslow Barracks was opened, which eventually became the main line. Hounslow Barracks was renamed Hounslow West on 1 December 1925.

Meanwhile, on 1 March 1880, the line was extended from West Brompton terminal to Putney Bridge, and on 3 June 1889 by means of running powers obtained from the London & South Western Railway this service was projected to Wimbledon.

As these services built up traffic, longer trains of nine carriages were introduced, which after 1879 became standard. The additional carriage was Second Class, and thereafter purchases of rolling stock were made in multiples of nine vehicles.

Lighting was provided from the beginning by coal gas supplied from mains established at Mansion House and Kensington High Street. The gas bags were arranged along the centre of the roof. In 1878 the Pintsch com-

10 *District 9-coach rake of steam stock at Ealing Broadway*   [11]

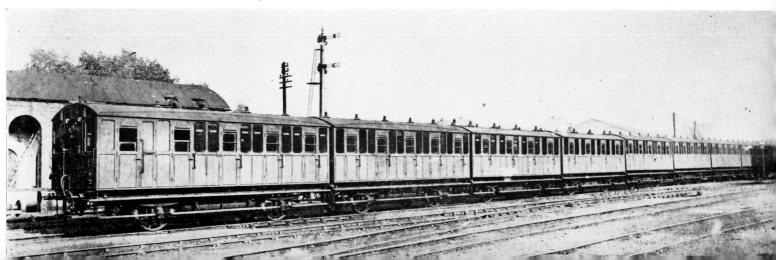

pressed oil gas was introduced, a plant being installed at Lillie Bridge to compress the gas to 90 lbs. per sq. in. The gas was stored in cylinders which were taken at night to suitable locations and connected to stand pipes. Each coach had a cylindrical wrought iron gas tank which was recharged at these stand pipes during the day as necessary. Subsequently, a main was laid from Lillie Bridge to

subsequent carriages from a number of builders. The original stock consisted of 152 carriages, but at the end of steam operation a total of 394 was owned.

The brakes originally fitted were of the Wilkins and Clark chain type, which were replaced first by the simple Westinghouse non-automatic brake and later by the fully-automatic Westinghouse.

Hammersmith to avoid the transfer of the gas cylinders to this point.

The vehicles were all 4-wheeled, having a length of 26 ft. 6 in. over the body frames and 29 ft. 2 in. over the buffers. The original vehicles were built by the Ashbury Railway Carriage Co., but the District bought its

11/12 *District Third Class steam brake coach and interior of compartment*

In the 1890s compartments were provided with a 'next station' indicator placed in a slot in the upper part of the partition between the compartments. It was originally operated by the guard pulling a string to display the plate bearing the name of the next station, but this was converted to a mechanical trip device placed on the track which automatically brought the plate with the name of the next station into view. The station names were interposed with advertisements but the equipment was not considered reliable because it required to be properly set at each terminal station, and if this were neglected, chaos resulted.

When the service originally began, about 12 departures an hour from Mansion House were operated, alternate trains going round the Inner Circle to Moorgate and to West Brompton. The Inner Circle service was shared with the Metropolitan. The Outer Circle service from Broad Street and Addison Road, operated by the London & North Western Railway, and the Great Western's Middle Circle service from Moorgate by way of Addison Road began in 1872. These services increased the number of trains to 16 an hour. When the District Line extensions were introduced the frequency went up to 19 an hour, which was the most that could be worked with steam traction.

The trains provided by the District for these services remained unchanged as to rolling stock types until electrification. At the end of steam operation the District fleet of 394 vehicles consisted of 215 Third Class, 92 Second Class, and 87 First Class coaches.

13 *District Railway locomotives awaiting scrapping at Ealing Common, after electrification*

4 | The Metropolitan extends to the country

The Metropolitan & St. John's Wood Railway, promoted in 1864, which had the Metropolitan Railway as a substantial shareholder, opened its line from Baker Street to Swiss Cottage on 13 April 1868. This line was only single-tracked with passing places at the four stations provided with double tracks. There were a number of short sections of steep gradients, especially the hump over the Regent's Canal, and to negotiate these difficulties

[14]

five powerful o–6–o tank locomotives built by the Worcester Engine Co. were purchased. However, these locomotives proved to be over-powered for the duty and when the Metropolitan had locomotives to spare because it had ceased, in 1871, to provide the motive power for the District Railway, they were sold (three in 1873; two in 1875) and the Beyer, Peacock 4–4–o type took up the duty.

At first a through service was provided from Swiss Cottage to Moorgate but in March 1869 this was discontinued. A through service to the City was not reinstated until after electrification.

The St. John's Wood Line reached West Hampstead on 30 June 1879, with an intermediate station at Finchley Road. Services began operating as far as Willesden Green in November the same year.

The extension beyond Willesden Green as far as Harrow

14 *A First Class Metropolitan Railway 'Jubilee' stock coach*

was opened to traffic on 2 August 1880. By this time it became clear that the single track between Swiss Cottage and Baker Street was totally inadequate. The single line had originally used human tokens to ensure line clear for passing trains. Later a wooden staff was issued to the train guard before he started his train. Two tracks over this section were completed by 10 July 1882, and shortly afterwards the St. John's Wood Railway ceased to exist as a separate corporate body, being absorbed by the Metropolitan Railway.

By 25 May 1885 the Metropolitan had extended to Pinner, Rickmansworth being reached on 1 September 1887. The line was pushed on towards Aylesbury which was connected to Baker Street by 1 September 1892. Meanwhile, the main line had reached Chalfont Road (since 1915 named Chalfont & Latimer) and this, to-gether with a single line branch from Chalfont Road to Chesham, came into use on 8 July 1889.

The Metropolitan continued to push out into the country by taking over the Aylesbury & Buckingham Railway (opened in 1868) so that by 1894 Verney Junction in the depths of Buckinghamshire had been reached. Through trains to this point from Baker Street began working on 1 January 1897, but local trains of the Metropolitan had run to Verney Junction from April 1894.

These extensions brought the need for more locomotives and between 1891 and 1901 the 'C', 'D', 'E' and 'F' classes appeared. The 'C' class were 0-4-4 tanks and four were built by Neilson & Co., similar to some contemporary engines constructed for the South Eastern Railway. The 'D' class which appeared in 1894 consisted of six engines by Sharp Stewart and were 2-4-0T type, similar to although not identical with a design used by the Barry Railway. The 'E' class were actually

15 *An 'E' class locomotive with a train composed of 'Dreadnoughts' with one 'Bogie' stock coach in 'Metroland', perhaps north of Pinner*

designed for the Metropolitan Railway, and out of the seven locomotives in the class three were built at Neasden, while the remainder were constructed by Hawthorn Leslie. The 'F' class built by the Yorkshire Engine Company were 0–6–2T, and apart from the wheel arrangement were similar to the 'E' class which were 0–4–4T type. Not all of these engines were fitted with condensing apparatus which was compulsory for tunnel operation south of Finchley Road.

The terminal track provided at Baker Street when the St. John's Wood Line was originally built was single, with a platform on both sides, and provided a running connection to the Circle Line. When these extensions called for a greater terminal capacity a track was provided on either side of the existing two platforms. In order to provide an easy interchange connection with the Circle Line without having to climb a stairway, a movable gangway was installed across the middle road which was only drawn back for empty rolling stock transfers to and from Edgware Road where the original Metropolitan locomotive shed and works were built.

Public demand caused the reintroduction of the through service after electrification, when the connection with the Circle Line was doubled and the gangway replaced by a drawbridge. The present arrangement and layout were not introduced until 1929 when Chiltern Court and the existing Baker Street station were completed.

Following some minor derailments with the original rolling stock a new 4-wheeled design was produced in 1887. Three complete trains of 9 vehicles were initially built by Craven Bros. of Sheffield. The bodies were 27 ft. 6 in. long over the ends, and had a wheelbase of 14 feet. There were two Second Class and two First Class coaches in the 9-vehicle rake and all were fitted with Smith's simple vacuum brake. The First Class coaches had four compartments while both the lower classes had five.

Each train was made up with two brake coaches, a Third Class at one end which had 3 compartments and a luggage compartment used in an emergency to carry 11 passengers on wooden benches alongside the guard. At the other end of the rake a Second Class brake coach had the normal 5 compartments, one of which was occupied by the guard and could accommodate 5 passengers as well.

These trains were not originally fitted with steam heating coils but this amenity was added later. However, the Pintsch high-pressure gas lighting system was installed when built. As the introduction of these vehicles coincided with the celebration of Queen Victoria's Jubilee they became known throughout their life as 'Jubilee Stock'.

To provide a service to Aylesbury a further four trains of this stock were purchased in 1892 from the same builders. They were delivered in 8-coach sets made up into two 4-coach portions allowing the trains to be divided at Chalfont Road (now Chalfont & Latimer) so that one portion could proceed to Chesham while the other went on to Aylesbury.

These sets had long buffers and screw couplings at the outer ends of the 4-coach portions. This uncoupling arrangement did not last long and the inner brake coaches were converted to standard types, but the formations remained at 8-coach length.

There were 59 of these coaches which became redundant at the time of electrification. However, some were rescued from the scrap heap and converted at Neasden Works to run with electric motive power over the electrified tracks to augment the service at peak periods. They were finally withdrawn in 1912.

5 | 'Bogie' Stock and the Chesham shuttle

It became obvious that the 4-wheeled and the rigid-wheelbase stock was unsatisfactory for the Extension services—the name given to the through workings to Rickmansworth, Chesham, Amersham, and beyond.

Between 1898 and 1900 54 vehicles were built which were variously known as 'Ashbury' Stock or 'Bogie' Stock. Four more were added later, bringing the total to 58.

The Ashbury Railway Carriage & Iron Co. of Manchester received the first order for four 6-coach trains equipped with bogies, the first on the Metropolitan. These trains went into service in 1898.

The bodies of the vehicles were 39 ft. 6 in. long but the overall length over buffers was 42 ft. 4¾ in. The width of the body frame was 8 ft. 3 in., but to clear the outside grab rails another 5 inches were needed. The total height of the body above rail level was 11 ft. 7 in., but a further 6 inches were required to clear the top of the 'torpedo' type ventilators.

Three classes of accommodation were provided with 10 seats in each compartment irrespective of class. The [17]

16 *'H' class locomotive with train containing a 4-wheeled brake van and a 'Bogie' stock vehicle as well as 'Dreadnoughts' leaving Harrow, about 1920*

rule in each compartment was five a side, but there were retractable armrests in the First Class compartments to permit this. The Second and Third Class coaches had 7 compartments but brake coaches were provided with 5 compartments in addition to a luggage compartment. The First Class coaches had 6 compartments giving more leg room for the passengers. The moquette upholstery was trimmed with lace and cord, but all the compartments had upholstery of some kind, although the Third Class was the most austere. The floors were deadened to reduce running noise by incorporating some felt as a lining above the steel floor plating. Spring blinds were fitted to the sidelights of all compartments and steam heating was supplied throughout.

For the first time on the Metropolitan this stock was equipped with electric lighting providing two lamps of 8-candle power in each compartment. A battery, connected to an axle-driven dynamo working on Stone's system, provided the power for this illumination. When the vehicles entered service, no passenger alarm was incorporated and this safety device was not installed until some time later, although the trains were fitted with the automatic vacuum brake system. The vehicles were fitted with pressed steel bogies at 25 ft. centres, each bogie having a 7 ft. wheelbase. Each wheel had two cast iron brake shoes, coupled by rigging to the vacuum brake cylinder.

The normal formation of these trains was:

$$B_2T–2T–1T–1/3T–3T–B_3T$$

which formed a rake 252 feet in length.

The First/Third composite coach had only 6 compartments and both the First and Third compartments were roomier than their counterparts on coaches all of one class.

As soon as the original sets were in service it was felt that some further trains of this type were required. The Metropolitan Railway intended to build some of them in its own workshops at Neasden, but pressure of work necessitated most of the order being placed with car-builders. Five additional train sets were ordered. One set was built by the Metropolitan Railway itself, two sets were constructed by Cravens of Sheffield, and two further sets were built by Ashbury, the original car-builders. The first of these additional sets went into service in 1900.

Until electrification, this stock maintained the through services to Chesham, Aylesbury, and Verney Junction from Baker Street.

The fleet of 'Bogie' stock was increased from 54 to 58 vehicles by the addition of four other vehicles at a later date—one in 1903, two in 1908 which had originally been used in electrification trials at Wembley Park in 1899, and a fourth in 1910.

When the electric train services on the Metropolitan Railway, south of Harrow, began in 1905, the need for steam passenger trains decreased. This not only rendered all the older rigid wheelbase stock redundant, but it also made some of the 'Bogie' stock surplus to daily requirements. Arrangements were then made for some of these vehicles to be converted for electric working, and between 1906 and 1924 all the 'Bogie' stock was converted to electric working. Initially some thought was given to providing trains of this kind for dual working, changing the motive power at the outskirts of the electrified area, but this proposal was abandoned and the 'Bogie' stock became part of the electric fleet which will be considered as such in due course. Apart from the provision of an equipment chamber and a driving cab the appearance of the vehicle was altered very little in the conversion. These trains continued to provide yeoman service within the

17 *The 'Bogie' stock retained for the Chesham shuttle service*

electrified area, principally on the Uxbridge line, and subsequently to Stanmore after this line was opened on 10 December 1932 and until 20 November 1939, when the Bakerloo took over this service.

The line was extended to Chesham on 8 July 1889, and for three years Chesham was the northern terminus of the Metropolitan Railway. After 1892 Chesham became the terminal of a branch which left the main line at Chalfont Road (later Chalfont & Latimer).

The need to provide a push-and-pull type shuttle train for the Chesham branch from Chalfont caused the life of six of the cars to be prolonged. Three dated from 1898, two from 1900, and one from 1899. These coaches were made up into two 3-car sets and each set was modified to provide a push-and-pull unit to work with a steam locomotive at [19] one end. To make them suitable for this duty the motor bogies were replaced by trailer bogies. The equipment was removed from the compartment, which reverted to a guard's van allowing the passenger accommodation to become four compartments. As originally built these coaches had two full-length stepboards, the lower one being at axle box level and the upper at the lower side of the solebar. These boards were removed when the stock was converted to electric working and only one replaced at the top side of the solebar. The steam locomotives for the push-and-pull operations were always supplied by the main line, at first the London & North Eastern Railway and afterwards British Railways. The engine pulled the train in the Chalfont direction, and pushed towards Chesham when the driver used the compartment in the leading coach modified to take the remote controls for the engine at the rear. The fireman always remained with the engine to attend to the fire and the boiler.

Originally, it was intended to have three push-and-pull sets for this service, as it was suggested that reversal should be arranged at Rickmansworth so that connection could be made with the electric train service terminating there rather than with the Aylesbury steam train at Chalfont & Latimer. To do this two trains in steam with one spare would have been required. As this proposal was not implemented only one shuttle in steam was necessary, and the second train remained as a spare. Each set spent a week in service, being normally changed over on Sunday, to allow maintenance to be carried out at Neasden Depot.

The final steam working on the Chesham branch was the last train on Sunday/Monday, 11/12 September 1960. This steam shuttle was replaced initially by a 3-car formation of 'T' stock and later 'P' stock and finally, when sufficient new stock was available, by a 4-car set of new 'A' stock.

In addition to these shuttle trains, which began working in 1941 and which run all day between Chalfont & Latimer and Chesham to connect with the Amersham trains, there are certain through trains in the peak hours to Baker Street.

The steam shuttle cars, however, obtained a further lease of life as four of the vehicles were acquired by the Bluebell Railway and one by British Railways for preservation and eventual exhibition.

6 | Metropolitan & Great Central Joint Committee and the 'Dreadnoughts'

On 1 July 1891 the Metropolitan Railway acquired the Aylesbury & Buckingham Railway, with which at that time it had no physical connection, as the main line did not reach Aylesbury until the following year. The Aylesbury & Buckingham line was reconstructed and the tracks were doubled. This work was completed by New Year's Day, 1897, and a through service of Metropolitan Line trains

this terminal the Great Central was granted running powers over the Metropolitan from Quainton Road to Canfield Place. The section of the Metropolitan Railway from Quainton Road to Verney Junction became virtually a branch line, although this point remained the out-of-town terminus for Metropolitan trains until 4 July 1936, when the passenger service beyond Quainton Road was withdrawn.

From Harrow, the Metropolitan constructed two additional tracks alongside its own, without any provision for station platforms, as far as Canfield Place near Finchley Road; tracks later leased to the Great Central. From Canfield Place into Marylebone, however, the Great Central constructed its own tracks. Great Central passen-

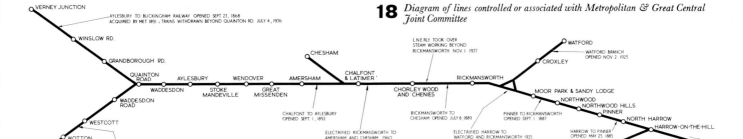

18 *Diagram of lines controlled or associated with Metropolitan & Great Central Joint Committee*

from Baker Street to Verney Junction was introduced.

The Manchester, Sheffield & Lincolnshire Railway obtained powers in 1893 for an extension to London, which eventually joined the Aylesbury & Buckingham Railway at Quainton Road in 1898. Since 1 August 1897 this railway had, in fact, been known as the Great Central Railway, providing the last main line terminal to be built in London, at Marylebone. In order to reach

ger trains ran into the new terminal at Marylebone on 15 March 1899, although the full track quadrupling south of Harrow was not completed until 1901.

The railway north of Harrow was served by two companies, and this was given legal recognition on 2 April 1906 by the formation of the Metropolitan & Great Central Joint Committee to which the line from Harrow-on-the-Hill to Verney Junction, including Chesham and

Brill, was leased. This Joint Committee then became responsible for all the Metropolitan lines outside the electrified area. The Metropolitan & Great Central Joint Committee never owned any passenger rolling stock; the service was provided either by Metropolitan or Great Central trains.

The development of the Great Central suburban services, with handsome trains of compartment stock, established a reputation for comfort and efficiency, which put even the new Metropolitan 'Bogie' stock in the shade. The Metropolitan Railway, therefore, had to look to its laurels, and designed a new class of stock for the non-electrified territory which was immediately given the sobriquet 'Dreadnought'. They were both longer and higher off the ground—or to be more technical, 'from rail level'—than previous stock. They were also provided

[22]

with semi-elliptical roofs. The fleet of Dreadnoughts eventually totalled 92, the last batch being built in 1923. Almost two-thirds of this total remained in service over the non-electrified lines of the Metropolitan until steam passenger service was eliminated on 9 September 1961 with the curtailment of the services of London Transport trains at Amersham.

The Dreadnoughts were 54 feet long having compartments with swing doors, provided with the familiar Metropolitan type rounded top to reduce damage if left open in the tunnels with restricted clearances. In addition the doorways were provided with draught excluders and the door locks with internal 'lift-to-open' type handles. These vehicles were 9 ft. 9 in. over stepboards. One unusual feature for compartment stock was that groups of three compartments were connected by a gangway. This arrangement was introduced to spread the passenger

19 *A 'Dreadnought' Third Class coach built by Metropolitan Amalgamated in 1912. Groups of three compartments were linked by a central corridor. (Metro-Cammell)*

20 *Central corridor in Third Class coach*

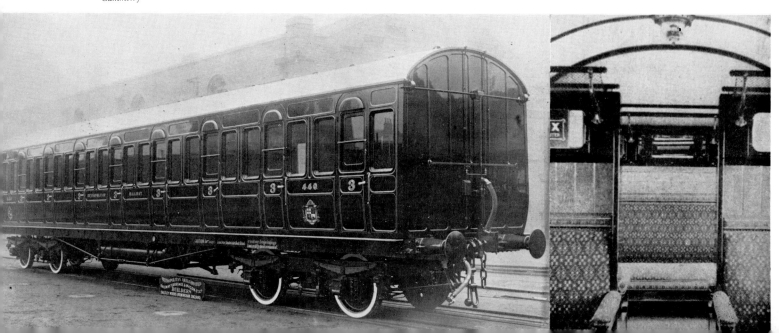

load in the peak hours and help to reduce the station stop times at busy stations.

The first two rakes of the Dreadnought stock were provided in loose-coupled sets of 5 vehicles made up in the formation:

B3T–3T–1T–1T–B3T

and were rebuilt in 1910 from redundant First Class control trailer cars built in 1905. These original vehicles were numbered from 419 to 428 in the Metropolitan number scheme, although there were four First Class coaches, four Third Class brake coaches, and two ordinary Third Class. These vehicles retained their numbers until they were withdrawn, as London Transport did not renumber the Metropolitan steam stock coaches. Twenty were built new in 1912, 42 in 1920, and a further 20 in 1923; some of these later vehicles were converted subsequently to electric working.

From the introduction of trains of this kind, only First and Third classes of accommodation were provided, as Second Class was finally withdrawn from all Metropolitan Railway trains on 17 December 1906. This formation of 5 coaches provided 112 First Class and 202 Third Class seats. There were 7 compartments in the First Class coaches and 9 compartments in 3 groups of 3 compartments in the Third Class. The intermediate partitions in the groups of 3 compartments were only provided as high as the top of the quarter lights. In the brake coaches, which had 7 compartments, some coaches had 2 groups of 3 compartments and one compartment with full partitions while it is understood that some brake coaches had a 2+3+2 arrangement. Doors were not provided in the gangway connecting the grouped compartments together.

The bogies, which were of pressed steel construction, had a wheelbase of 7 feet set at 35 ft. centres. The wheels, with full size tyres, were 36 inches in diameter.

The coaches were fitted with screw couplings and side buffers similar to those standardized in main line practice, and were equipped with automatic vacuum brakes. These trains were the first in Metropolitan Railway service to provide a passenger emergency alarm system; when the chain passing through each compartment was pulled, a valve in the vacuum brake pipe opened. This arrangement continued until the withdrawal of the vehicles.

The provision of steam coach heating and comfortable interiors made these vehicles of high standard, but they were not initially provided with electric lighting. The original trains of this stock were still equipped with Pintsch gas lighting using incandescent mantles instead of fantail burners. They were not converted to Stone's electric lighting system until 1918. The lighting control with this system retained pull-bar controls at the ends of the coaches.

More powerful steam locomotives were now required. The 'G' class 0–6–4T type, of which four were built by the Yorkshire Engine Co., appeared in 1916, and these engines all received names as well as numbers. Eight 'H' class with a 4–4–4T wheel arrangement built by Kerr Stuart came in 1921. The last steam engines built for the Metropolitan Railway were six 'K' class built in 1925 by Armstrong Whitworth, from parts originally made at Woolwich Arsenal. They were by far the largest and most powerful engines built for the Metropolitan Railway and were confined to duties north of Finchley Road, as they were out of gauge for tunnel working. The engines were 2–6–4T type and were mostly used on freight workings. The 'G', 'H', and 'K' class locomotives were transferred to London & North Eastern Railway ownership on 1 November 1937, when

[23]

this railway took over responsibility for the motive power for all goods and passenger trains north of Rickmansworth.

[24]   After the electrification extension to Rickmansworth,

trains composed of 'Dreadnought' vehicles provided the steam stock trains running to Aylesbury and beyond. Subsequently the formation became 6 coaches, which was the standard train at the time of the withdrawal of steam-operated services, although some 7-coach trains

21 *An 'H' class locomotive with a 6-coach train of 'Dreadnought' stock climbing Chorley Wood bank*

22 ABOVE—*'Lord Aberconway', a 'G' class locomotive, together with a Westinghouse-type electric locomotive*

23 BELOW—*An 'H' class locomotive and a Metropolitan-Vickers-type electric locomotive*

were worked.

These trains were hauled by electric locomotives within the electrified territory and were criticized for causing delay to the service. This was partly due to the fact that the electric locomotives, with their short span for the collector shoes, became gapped at the numerous crossings particularly at Baker Street, Neasden, and Wembley Park. These conditions made it necessary for the driver to shut off power to avoid snatching the couplings, and to prevent arcing. Complaints were, in fact, received during the First World War of violent flashing from these trains, infringing the black-out regulations, and experiments were then conducted providing a bus line to connect additional collector shoes further down the train to the locomotive. The shoes were provided on the brake coaches so that one set was at the extreme end of the train.

This power bus line, which required jumper couplings between vehicles, was only provided on one side—the 'down' side (to use the Metropolitan Railway parlance), which thus made the brake coaches 'handed' so that they could only work at the 'down' or 'up' ends of the rakes. In general railway parlance the track leading to London was the 'up' track and that leading from London the 'down' track, so the 'down' side would be the left-hand side of a coach looking at it from the London end and the brake coach at the London end of the train would be at the 'up' end of the train. A small number of brake coaches were provided with bus line connections on both sides at the coupling end of the coach, so that by using the turntable provided at Neasden these coaches could be used at either end of the rakes.

The trains, however, still remained only steam heated although they spent at least a quarter of their operating time within the electrified territory. A steam locomotive was required to heat the coils before the coaches entered service, but in 1921 arrangements were made to fit electric heaters.

From 1930 onwards the gangway joining the three compartments on those early coaches was eliminated to give additional seating. The final delivery of 'Dreadnought' stock enabled the Bogie coaches to be converted to electric working. Later it became the turn of the 'Dreadnoughts' to be converted for electric working as the general design of the electric coaching stock, which later became known as the 'T' stock, was basically similar. Conversions of the 'Dreadnoughts' began in 1927. When electrification beyond Rickmansworth was planned it was intended that all the 'Dreadnought' vehicles should be converted to electric working. The Second World War, however, curtailed the conversion and a number of these coaches ended their days purely as steam stock vehicles.

After the formation of London Transport two significant changes were made; the bogies were changed to the 'K2' type as these became available from scrapped District Line cars. Subsequently, in 1953, the outer ends of the brake coaches were painted red.

7 | Electrification—experimentation

The success of electric traction on the City & South London Railway encouraged both the Metropolitan and the District managements to give consideration to the improvement of travel conditions, especially on the Inner Circle. A proposal in 1896 that the Inner Circle service should be hauled by electric locomotives to eliminate the smoke nuisance was seriously considered. One of the few things that the Metropolitan and the District managements agreed about at this time was that any electrification proposals should be undertaken on a common system.

The Metropolitan Railway carried out its own electrification experiments at Wembley Park, but in 1898 joined the District in financing a joint experiment on the latter company's line from High Street Kensington to Earl's Court. A temporary generating station was built at Warwick Road, Earl's Court. Power was provided at 600 volts DC and supplied to two conductor rails arranged one on either side of the running rails. The position of these rails was $12\frac{1}{2}$ inches from the gauge line (the gauge line being the inner edge of the nearest running rail) with the top surface for the collector shoe, contact being made at a position 3 inches above the top of the running rails. The provision of two conductor rails was probably arranged for two reasons. First, it was to avoid the need to improve the conductivity of the running rails through the fish plates and crossing connections and, secondly, to avoid interference with the block signalling

apparatus by stray earth currents if the conductivity of the running rails were bad.

After considering the conversion of existing rolling stock for the experiment it was decided to purchase a brand new 6-car train specially for the purpose. After numerous design arguments between the two railways a contract was placed with Brown, Marshalls & Company in May 1899, and it is interesting to note that the cars took only four months to construct, after which electrical [27]

24 *Diagram of rail positions*

EARL'S COURT EXPERIMENT

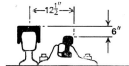

GREAT NORTHERN & CITY

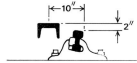

L.T. STANDARD

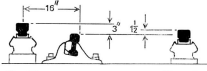

Positive   Negative

equipment was installed by Siemens Bros. at the District Railway Works at Lillie Bridge.

This 6-coach train consisted of two motor coaches and four trailer coaches. The trailers were not all identical; two contained 6 compartments and the other two 7 compartments. The motor coaches had a central gangway and a guard's compartment. The vehicles were lit by electric lamps, fed in series groups from the traction supply. Although up to this time the Metropolitan had been an advocate of the vacuum brake, the District's preference for the Westinghouse automatic brake prevailed.

The motor coaches were each equipped with four gearless motors, one on each axle, provided with 4 poles; 48-inch diameter wheels were fitted to enable the motor case to clear the track and this, in turn, necessitated the car underframe being raised about 6 inches over the bogies. The carbody floor was raised over the bogies and access was gained to this part of the vehicle where seats were provided by steps from the centre position. The bogies had a 7 ft. wheelbase.

Although a bus line was provided through the train, connecting all the collector shoes together on both motor coaches, no through control lines were provided, so that only the motor coach at the leading end was powered when the train was in motion. It is understood that one of the original conceptions of the proposed electrification scheme for the Inner Circle line was the provision of only one motor coach per train, fitted with a driving cab at both ends. This vehicle would then have been required to run round the train like a locomotive to reverse.

The four traction motors were controlled by a large spoked wheel which directly operated the switching contacts giving series, series-parallel and parallel combinations. Although electric braking was being incorporated into tram car control designs at this time, braking was performed by a separate air brake control handle.

The motor coaches carried an air compressor to supply the air brake, sanding gear and the whistle with power. A voltmeter and an ammeter were also provided as part of the cab equipment, since the driver had to ensure that the current being taken did not exceed a certain maximum before selecting the next notch on the wheel controller.

The train ran for the first time on Saturday, 9 December 1899, and began an experimental service on 14 May 1900. The fare was 1/-, later reduced to 6d., although it would seem that all three classes of accommodation were provided in the coaches.

The train was finally withdrawn from service on 6 November 1900 and the cars stored. Three became the property of the Metropolitan and three of the District. The District sold its vehicles to the Colne Valley & Halstead Railway while the Metropolitan placed the two trailer cars into the 'Bogie' stock fleet. The fate of the Metropolitan motor coach is not known.

The experiment appears to have been successful and both railways began plans for general electrification. The basic system of the experiment had been that of low-voltage direct current, rail-collected, at a potential of 500/600 volts which was already proving successful in America. This basic system had been adopted in London for the City & South London Railway and had just been installed on the new Central London Railway.

However, tenders were invited in 1900 from a number of electrical contractors and nine different concerns submitted proposals. Messrs. Ganz & Co. of Budapest proposed a 3,000-volt 3-phase alternating current system, and this tender was considered to be the most attractive. This system would have involved the use of two overhead wires insulated from each other with separate collecting devices for each wire, whilst the third phase would have been provided by the running rails. It is difficult, in retrospect, to understand the special attractiveness of this tender because at that time no electric railway was operating under such a system although one was under construction in Italy. Initially the scheme was accepted by the joint electrification committee of both railways, but the District subsequently withdrew its acceptance because by this time Charles Tyson Yerkes, the American traction financier, had acquired control. Yerkes's engineering advisers were not at all in favour of adopting an untried arrangement, in spite of the attractive price. The matter eventually was taken to arbitration.

The arbitration tribunal was headed by the Hon. Alfred Lyttelton, K.C. The Metropolitan nominee was Thomas Parker and the District was represented by H. F. Parshall. After a hearing lasting about three weeks the award, made in December 1901, was in favour of the low-voltage direct current system.

The Metropolitan Railway had, by an Act of 1898, obtained powers to work its railway by electric traction and had conducted experiments at Wembley Park, quite independent of the joint experiment at Earl's Court. These experiments had been conducted under the direction of Thomas Parker, so that he was already very familiar with the general problems involved.

Several learned gentlemen of the era gave evidence before the tribunal, many being in fact in favour of the high voltage AC system because it was thought that considerable difficulty would be experienced in providing an adequate supply of continuous current (as DC was then known) at a potential of only 500 volts. There was available at this time a lot of experience with 500-volt tramway systems, where it was the practice to use an

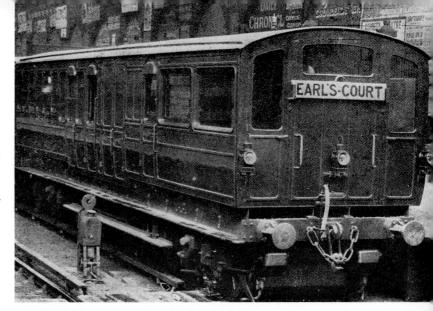

25 *The experimental electric train at Earl's Court in 1900*

overhead wire conductor for one polarity and the running rails for the other. It had been determined quite early that the troubles arising from earth leakage by such a system were minimized by making the overhead wire positive and the earth return through the running rails negative. In tramway systems the voltage drop was limited to 7 volts to reduce the troubles caused by earth leakages, the electrolysis of water and gas mains, and especially telegraph systems. It was obvious that this limitation would apply to underground railways, especially the Inner Circle which was only just below street level. This factor was going to be a very onerous requirement involving the use of negative boosters to reduce the running rail voltage drop. The leakage current from an alternating current supply, especially of a 3-phase system, would have caused negligible damage and this

[29]

factor was one of the main points considered. The provision of two 'third' rails or the fourth rail system finally adopted avoided the necessity of meeting the 7-volt requirement in the running rails, and this system became standard for both the District and Metropolitan Railways and subsequently for London Transport.

Because of limited clearances the rail placed outside the running rails was fixed at 16 inches from the gauge line of the nearer running rail, but it was decided to place the rail of the other polarity in the centre of the track, which minimized the loss of supply at junctions and crossings. The normal arrangement is for the rail at the outside of the running rails to be at positive polarity with the surface contact 3 inches above the running rail level, and the centre rail at negative polarity having surface contact $1\frac{1}{2}$ inches above the running rail.

8 | The original District electrification— The first 'A' Stock

The District Railway determined to eliminate steam working altogether, while on the other hand the Metropolitan, with its country services, had a programme which limited electric traction to the more congested inner area, leaving the extension services to be worked by steam.

The Ealing & South Harrow Railway was incorporated in 1894 to build a line from South Harrow to join the District Railway at Hanger Lane. The railway was completed and fit for steam traffic in 1899, but no passenger service was operated. In 1900 this separate railway, which had not owned any rolling stock, was absorbed by the District and it was decided that the initial electrification work should be undertaken on this line.

A temporary generating station was constructed at Alperton near the Grand Union Canal, using the plant from the Earl's Court experiment, to supply power until the District Railway power house then being constructed at Lots Road, Chelsea, was opened.

The District at this time also electrified the tracks from Hanger Lane junction to Acton Town (then known as Mill Hill Park). The line, using electric traction from Mill Hill Park to Park Royal with a station at North Ealing, was brought into operation on 23 June 1903 to provide a service for the Royal Agricultural Show which opened that day in the fields near that station. Five days later a service through to South Harrow began. The line to South Harrow was used to try out different equipment on the rolling stock and to train motormen for the general electrification then under way.

The 'A' class comprised two 7-car trains built by the Brush Electrical Engineering Co. of Loughborough. The cars were 50¼ feet long and were basically of American design, bearing a striking resemblance to cars constructed about the same time for the Interborough Rapid Transit Company of New York. The choice of a 7-car train length seems to have been made because it was considered at the time that this was the maximum length of train which could be accommodated on the District Railway generally, without lengthening the station platforms.

These 7-car trains as originally constructed contained three motor cars and four trailer cars. The leading motor cars were different from those in the middle. The leading cars were provided with luggage compartments just behind the driving cabs and at the other end a platform with gates. The middle motor cars originally had gates at both ends with fold-up driving seats and a cabinet containing the master controller and brake valve, so that these cars could be driven from either end and operated as a single vehicle if necessary. The 7-car trains could be divided into smaller formations depending upon the position of the middle motor car.

The bodies were 8 ft. 4 in. wide and had straight sides constructed of fireproofed wood, the roofs being lined with asbestos to reduce the fire risk. The appearance was enhanced by the provision of arched window frames. The leading motor cars had seats for 38 passengers, while the middle motor cars had 48, all in longitudinal seats, whereas the trailer cars seated 52 with some transverse seats. All the seats were finished in rattan. Various external colour schemes seem to have been adopted but that best remembered by those old enough was a bright yellow picked out with maroon. No First Class accommodation was provided on these cars, but all were fitted with centrally-placed hand-operated sliding doors, in addition to the gates on the end platforms.

A special shed was built at South Harrow to look after the new electric rolling stock, and the new cars had their electrical equipment installed there.

One train was equipped with B.T.H. Type GE68 equipment and traction motors identical with those then operating on the Interborough Rapid Transit in New York. The other train was equipped with Westinghouse traction motors and control gear similar to those then in use on the Brooklyn Elevated of New York.

The B.T.H. equipment consisted of individual electro-magnetic contactors controlled directly from the 600-volt traction supply. This system was known at the time as the Sprague–Thomson–Houston System.

The Westinghouse arrangement used a low-voltage storage battery (14 volts) to provide the control, the driver's master control handle being a miniature thumb switch which provided three positions, shunting, series, and parallel, giving automatic acceleration under the control of a current limit switch.

Under the control of the low-voltage supply from the master controller, a circular contact drum underneath the car was notched by a pawl and ratchet system each time the current relay was released, accelerating the motors. Although the Westinghouse arrangements had a number of technical advantages such as low-voltage control, automatic acceleration, and a simple dead man's control, the B.T.H. equipment proved more reliable and was adopted by the District as standard. The Westinghouse cars were subsequently converted.

Even the braking system of the two trains was different. The Westinghouse train was naturally fitted with the associated Westinghouse air brake, while the B.T.H. train was originally equipped with the Christensen brake. These two systems were not dissimilar in their action, but the Westinghouse system proved the more reliable and was adopted as standard.

The trains were originally provided with sanding gear and it was understood this was needed from time to time to get up the Ealing Common bank. However, this apparatus was disconnected when it was found that too generous an application of sand to the rails interfered with the track circuits associated with the new automatic signalling system. This was a development of that first introduced in 1901 on the Boston Elevated Railway. Track circuit signalling was materially assisted by the use of the fourth rail traction system, which left the running rails clear of traction current so that they could be utilized exclusively for signalling requirements. The system required the running rails to be divided into insulated sections by means of block joints. A train or just a pair of wheels on any section caused the two running rails to be shorted together detecting the presence of a train. Incorporated with the track circuit was the train stop and tripcock. When a signal was at danger the train stop was raised and should the approaching train overrun, the tripcock would come in contact with the train stop, the brakes then being auto-matically applied. This system, apart from the problems caused by sanding, was very successful and was adopted throughout the District, over the congested parts of the Metropolitan, and subsequently on the Tube lines as well.

These cars later had a centrally-placed automatic coupler which was designed by an American engineer, one of the team directing the electrification. This mechanical coupler, known throughout the next half-century as the 'Ward', has perpetuated its designer's name because it became the standard coupling used by the Underground group of companies until the advent of completely automatic couplers. The Ward coupler only coupled the cars mechanically, as the electrical and pneu-matic connections had to be completed by hand. At uncoupling it was necessary to unlatch both locking pawls by means of a shunting pole.

Subsequently some of the 'A' class trailer cars were converted to control trailers by the provision of half a cab at one of the gate ends. The leading bogies of these cars were then fitted with shoegear. The trains had a continuous bus line so that the provision of shoes on control trailers enabled two and three car trains to be

26 *The original electric rolling stock depot at South Harrow, 1903*

27 *Original 'A' stock train at South Harrow. The 'right-hand' side driving position of this B.T.H.-equipped electric train should be specially noted*

operated without the motor car becoming gapped. The collector shoes were originally suspended from the ends of wooden frames attached to the sides of the trucks. This arrangement was not satisfactory and it was replaced by a shoebeam suspended between the axle boxes.

The American influence set the pattern for the Underground group of companies. The vehicles were known as cars instead of carriages and the bogies became trucks. In addition the practice generally adopted in New York

of having only one motor truck per motor car became standard on the District for a long time.

The 'A' stock were confined throughout their life to operating at first the shuttle from Mill Hill Park (now Acton Town) to South Harrow and then, in 1905, from South Acton to Hounslow. The South Harrow shuttle trains were extended to Uxbridge over the Metropolitan Railway by the connection from South Harrow to Rayners Lane on 1 March 1910. The 'A' stock cars were finally withdrawn in 1925.

9 | The District 'B' Stock

In August 1903, following the successful operation of the South Harrow Line by electric traction, the District Railway placed orders for 420 new cars to electrify the whole system. These cars were to provide sixty 7-car trains, 12 containing four motor cars and 48 with three [34] motor cars. The trains with four motor cars were intended to divide at Mill Hill Park (now Acton Town) into two portions, 4 cars to Ealing Broadway and 3 cars to Hounslow, each with two motor cars. However, this type of service did not materialize and the Hounslow service was maintained for many years by a shuttle working from South Acton composed of 'A' stock. Actually, from 6 April 1906, the working of 7-car trains virtually ceased, the standard formation being a 6-car train with three motor cars.

The new cars followed the basic American design with B.T.H. traction equipment and GE69 type traction motors, arising from the experience on the South Harrow operations. Much to the chagrin of the English car-building industry, the order for 280 of these cars was

28 *A motor car of 'A' stock at South Harrow about 1903, showing trailer-end with gates*

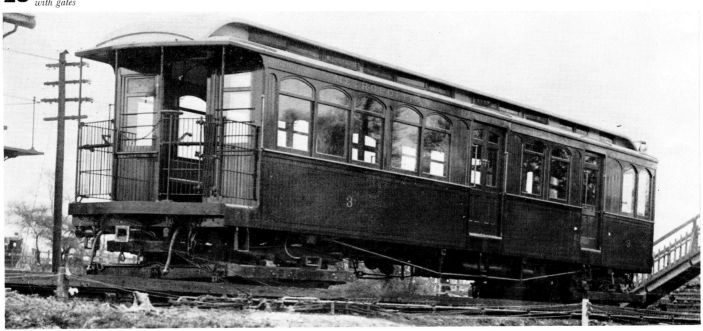

placed with a French syndicate headed by Les Ateliers de Construction Du Nord de la France, with works at Blanc Misseron. Some of the cars (mostly the trailers) were, however, built at other works in France at Pantin, Ivry, St. Denis, and Lunéville, each firm building its own bogies. The 140 cars built in England were constructed by Brush of Loughborough and the Metropolitan Amalgamated at its Ashbury and Lancaster Works.

All the cars were to be delivered by 1905 to what was originally known as the Mill Hill Park Works, which became Ealing Common Works but was later reduced to the status of a Depot after the completion of Acton Works in 1922. This depot had been constructed by the District Railway to look after the new electric rolling stock. Lillie Bridge, the original District Locomotive Works and Depot, was subsequently adapted in 1906 to look after

29 *Brush-built motor car of 'B' stock with luggage compartment showing the original fine lining of the main panelling as delivered in 1905. The car is also fitted with the original cast steel bogies, the trailer bogie not being provided with shoegear*

the Piccadilly tube trains.

Both the English and Continental carbuilders were behind in deliveries. In spite of this electric services were

[35]

30 *A Metropolitan Amalgamated built 'B' stock motor car on the traverser at Acton Works after conversion to take an A2 motor bogie*

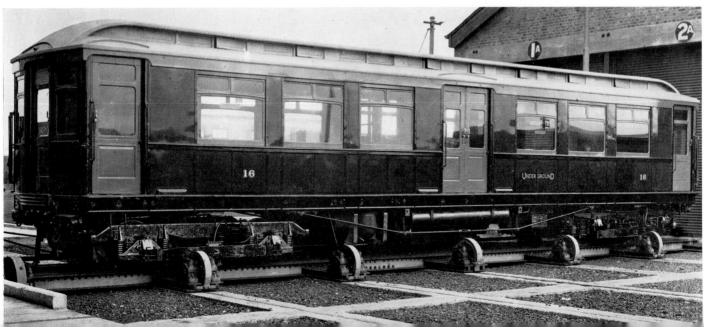

31 *The vestibule ends of 'B' stock. The pantograph protection barrier was not fitted to subsequent stock. Passengers were supposed to enter by the end doors and leave by the middle doors, which necessitated the sign above the doorway*

inaugurated on 13 June 1905 between South Acton and Hounslow. A through service from Whitechapel to Ealing was operated by electric traction for the first time on 1 July 1905.

After delivery from the carbuilders the electrical equipment for the new cars was installed at Ealing Common. This was of the well-tried Sprague–Thomson–Houston electro-magnetic type, one equipment on each

motor car controlling two traction motors of the GE69 type placed in one motor truck; the other bogie of the motor cars was a trailer truck but carried collector shoegear.

The cars had wooden bodies 49 ft. $6\frac{1}{2}$ in. long with a width of 8 ft. $10\frac{1}{2}$ in. at the cant rail. Ventilators in the clerestory roof could be opened by means of a lever provided in the end vestibule. Rush-hour seats, of the flap type, were also installed originally in the end vestibules but these were later removed.

The cars were provided with double doors at the centre and single sliding doors at the end vestibules. These doors were originally fitted with pneumatic cylinders placed at the top of the doors to allow control by the gateman who rode on the car. Opening and closing was effected by means of a 4-way cock manipulated by the conductor or gateman. This system did not work very well, being referred to at the time as a mechanical monstrosity. It was subsequently removed, the doors then being hand operated, with the double doors becoming a balanced pair—that is, the opening of one leaf of the pair automatically opened the other leaf. The original scheme of operation was for the end doors to be used for entrance and the middle doors for exit, but at times of heavy

32 *Interior of a 'B' stock class end motor car with all longitudinal seats, original armrests and rattan upholstery*

33 *Interior of a 'B' class middle motor car after retrimming with moquette seating, probably following its conversion to a trailer car*

traffic this arrangement was impossible to control even with a conductor on every car. Communicating doors between the cars were provided over the middle buffers. These doors had windows with etched designs including the car number but once these windows were broken, or had to be replaced for any reason, plain glass was inserted.

Of the original 420 cars, 192 were motor cars and 228 were trailers. There were three types of motor car: end motor cars with a luggage compartment, end motor cars without a luggage compartment, and middle motor cars. The cars with a luggage compartment placed immediately behind the driver had a saloon seating 40 passengers. Only 20 cars were originally built in this way and these were subsequently reconstructed, converting the luggage space for passenger use.

The end motor cars without a luggage compartment had seats for 48 passengers entirely in longitudinally facing seats. There were originally 100 cars constructed in this way.

The middle motor cars were provided with driving positions at both ends and two sets of companion seats in the middle of the body, which enabled these cars also to seat 48, within the passenger saloon. There were originally 72 cars of this type.

The trailer cars were similar in layout to the middle motor cars but they were built entirely of wood, while the motor cars had steel underframes on which the wooden bodies were constructed.

Three of the original motor cars were scrapped after being involved in collisions. The first one to be scrapped was in 1909 after an accident at Ealing Broadway. The train had entered service from Ealing Common Depot, running empty to Ealing Broadway to take up passenger working, and ran into the buffer stops with fatal result to a

34 *The original lifting shop at Acton Works, in 1922. A GE69 motor is being lowered into an early-type motor bogie*

member of the crew. This accident arose from insufficient air being available to apply the brakes at a terminal station with buffer stops, and caused the introduction of one of the fundamental safety features on London's Underground, namely the control governor. The control governor then devised prevented forward movement of a train if insufficient air was available in the brake pipe to provide an efficient brake application. This equipment

[37]

is now always installed as part of the safety control in all Underground trains.

In 1923 forty-two of the motor cars were converted to trailer cars when the 'G' class cars arrived. Later, in the 1928/29 District Line modernization programme, a further 110 motor cars were converted to trailer cars, but at this time some of the wooden trailer cars were scrapped. This conversion left only 37 of the original motor cars operating as such and at this time the original GE69 traction motors which had no interpoles were replaced with GE212 type, available when the Watford Joint Stock was scrapped in 1930.

Of the 228 trailer cars, 32 were fitted with master controllers to enable them to act as control trailers. These vehicles were mainly used on the shuttle services to Hounslow, South Harrow, Uxbridge, and sometimes on the Putney Bridge–Edgware Road service. Half of these control trailers survived until the general scrapping of the 'B' stock under the 1935/40 New Works programme. The trailer cars were scrapped in batches according to their condition, some when 1923 stock entered service, but the majority after the 1927/28 programme when most of the motor cars were converted to trailer cars. These cars, now trailers but orginally motor cars, were themselves displaced in the 1935/40 New Works programme and scrapped.

As originally built, a type of pantograph barrier was provided to prevent passengers slipping or falling between the cars. These were later removed. The interiors had a box-like appearance as very small windscreens were provided at the narrow centre doorways. The motorman's cab formed part of the end vestibule. The motor-

[38]

35 *View of Ealing Common Depot from the Ealing end about 1921. 'B' stock vehicles in the foreground with some new 'F' stock on 9 road*

man was screened off by a partition. This half of the vestibule could not be used by passengers. The longitudinal seats were not originally provided with armrests; this was a subsequent addition to ensure a fair distribution of the seating. The seats themselves were covered with rattan in the Third Class, and plush in the First Class. Eighteen carbon filament lamps provided the illumination, a very meagre form of lighting in comparison with present-day standards.

In addition to the clerestory roof ventilators, small side lights above the main lights could be pushed up by releasing a spring catch.

The original motor bogie of cast steel construction of American design, having a wheelbase of 6 ft. 6 in., carried the two GE69 traction motors. This bogie, designated the 'A' type, was not very satisfactory, fractures of the members being common and repairs being executed by thermit welding. Some of the 1905 motor cars were re-equipped with a plate and angle riveted type of truck which was designated the 'A2'. This bogie became the standard for District Line motor cars for many years. These replacement bogies were constructed by the Leeds Forge Company.

The original trailer bogie suffered from the same basic defects. This bogie, designated the 'K' type, was of equalizer bar construction and was replaced by the 'K2' constructed of plate and angles. This 'K2' bogie was one of the most successful ever designed, being practically trouble-free for its entire life, so much so that it was retained for further use on Metropolitan steam stock coaches and Circle Line trailer cars when the 1905 District cars were scrapped.

The 'A2' and 'K2' bogies were heavier than the original type and a 'B' class motor car weight increased from 31·7 tons to 35 tons when fitted with the improved bogies. The brake power was also improved as the original trailer truck was only provided with single block rigging, whereas the 'K2' bogie had clasp-type double block brake rigging on all wheels.

[39]

36 *Type 'A' motor bogie without shoebeams fitted originally to 'B' stock*

10 The Metropolitan early Electric Stock

The Metropolitan, unlike the District, placed a number of separate orders for its rolling stock to cover the services to be electrified. There were a number of fundamental differences in the basic design of these cars compared with those ordered by the District.

The Metropolitan decided to have motor cars with two motor bogies, two sets of traction equipments, and four traction motors. The District motor cars had only one set of equipment, one motor bogie with two traction motors, and one trailer bogie. The Metropolitan vehicles, although open saloon type, were not originally provided with centre doors.

An order for 50 trailer cars was placed in 1902 with Brown Marshalls, but it was not until six months later that the Metropolitan Amalgamated Railway Carriage & Wagon Co., which had meanwhile absorbed Brown Marshalls, received an order for 20 motor cars. This delay in ordering the motor cars may have been due to the difficulty in deciding the type of electrical equipment to be installed.

In 1904 another contract was placed with the Metropolitan Amalgamated for 36 motor cars and 62 trailer cars, with an option for a further 20 motor cars and 40 trailer cars at the same price if ordered within a specified time. In the event, this option was taken up with the purchase of six additional motor cars making a total fleet of 82 motor cars, 76 First Class trailer cars, and 76 Third Class trailer cars, providing 38 6-car trains with six spare motor cars.

The original cars were 52 ft. 6 in. long over the buffers, with a body width of 8 ft. 9 in. The motor cars had a full width cab at the leading end with an open platform enclosed by iron work at the trailing end, while the trailer cars had open platforms at both ends. The gates in the iron work at the platform side were controlled by levers operated by a gateman who could stand on the central buffer between the cars. The space between the gates on the platform side was protected by a 'lazy-tong' type barrier which was fixed to each car, adjacent barriers being fixed together when the cars were coupled.

The original 70 cars were intended to provide 10 × 7-car trains, but due to inadequate platform lengths the train formation adopted was of six cars. The standard forma-

[40]

37 *A 1905 motor car. This car was later renumbered 2526 and the luggage compartment was removed*

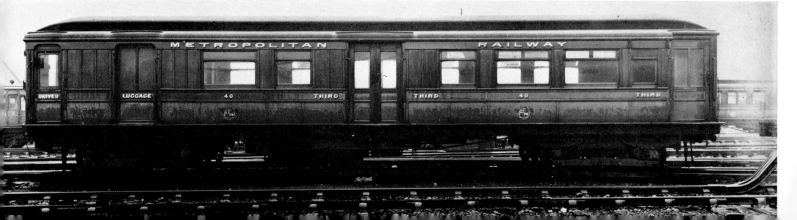

tion was then 3M–3T–1T–1T–3T–3M, all the motor cars providing Third Class accommodation. There were then 10 trailer cars surplus, and when the second batch of cars to make up 18×6-car trains was ordered, allowance was made to incorporate these 10 trailer cars from the original order.

By this time, however, a further complication had arisen. Two of the 10 trailer cars had been delivered with end vestibules instead of gates. In order to match the eight trailer cars with gates, a further eight motor cars and eight trailer cars were constructed with gates. There were then 14×6-car trains with gates.

Public service began on the Baker Street to Uxbridge Line on 4 July 1904, but with steam traction. Beginning on 1 January 1905 some of the services were being operated by electric traction, and by 20 March 1905 the whole of the Uxbridge service was maintained by electric rolling stock.

By 1906 it was decided that gate ends were entirely unsuitable for service conditions involving operation in the open, and a scheme of conversion to end vestibules was undertaken. Some of the cars were converted at Neasden Works, but a contract was placed with the Metro. Co. for the modification of the bulk of the vehicles.

The cars were originally coupled in train sets by means of a plain link and pin, but the outer ends of the motor cars were provided with screw couplings. This type of block formation was considered a disadvantage, and the cars were fitted with automatic mechanical couplings operating on similar principles to the District Ward coupling but not compatible with it. This coupling was known as the 'Buck Eye' and remained standard on Metropolitan Railway electric rolling stock.

It is understood that some difficulty arose with the Board of Trade Inspecting Officer concerning the proposals to work short trains from Harrow to Uxbridge in the off-peak, made up of three cars propelled in passenger service in one direction with the driver in the motor car in the rear. The objection was overcome by the provision of 'driving' trailer cars by equipping the first class trailer cars with a cab position and master controllers. The term 'driving trailer' was used thereafter by the Metropolitan Railway for this type of car, while the District and Tube Railways used the term 'control trailer' for a vehicle performing this type of duty.

As originally built the cars were of the saloon type with end vestibules or platforms but without centre doorways, typical of American design of the period. Behind the driving cab in the motor car a luggage compartment was provided which had a sliding door into the passenger saloon. This saloon had seats for 48 passengers, which were arranged 24 longitudinally and 24 in three bays of double transverse.

The trailer cars had seats for 56 with three transverse bays in the centre and eight longitudinal seats on either side at each end. Double sliding doors were provided at the passenger gangway ends of the cars to gain access to the vestibules. Only two classes of accommodation were provided, with buffalo-hide seat covering in the Third Class and moquette in the First Class.

The lighting was arranged from the traction current supply with circuits of 5 lamps of 32 candle power in each series. In all, 20 lamps were fitted in pendants in the clerestory roofs, or from the cant rails—no shades were provided. About 4 kw. of heating from tubular resistance heaters were provided in motor cars, with a slight increase in the trailer cars.

The electrical equipment for the first batch of cars was ordered from the British Westinghouse Electric & Manufacturing Co. of Trafford Park. Each motor car was fitted with four Westinghouse type 50M traction motors providing about 150 h.p. each. They were 4-pole machines, nose suspended in the truck frames but had split motor cases. This motor drove the axle on which it was mounted by means of spur gearing with a ratio of 17/54, the motored wheels being 36 inches in diameter when new.

The traction control was the early Westinghouse electro-pneumatic type with the so-called 'turret' controller. The electro-pneumatic switches were arranged in a circle around a large coil which acted as a blow-out or arc-suppressing device for the main switch contacts. The multiple unit control of these turret controllers was arranged by means of a low-voltage circuit fed from a 14-volt lead-acid battery. This battery arrangement was replaced in 1908 by a small motor generator set, driven by the traction supply, and subsequently all Westinghouse equipped motor cars were fitted with two of these motor generator sets. Changeover switches to select either set could be operated by the driver when necessary.

All the motor cars of the second batch were equipped with similar Westinghouse equipments, but by this time some dissatisfaction was being expressed as to its reliability

and consideration was being given to adopting the B.T.H. type of equipment favoured by the District Railway. The troubles with the Westinghouse equipments in fact resulted in the complete replacement of the turret controllers with a straight contactor bank of electro-pneumatic switches. Conversion to this type of equipment actually began in 1906.

Arising from the repair problems affecting motor cars it was evident that to keep trains in service some additional spare motor cars were required. An order for six additional motor cars was placed in September 1905, but the order for six motor car sets of Westinghouse equipment was cancelled in favour of a similar number of B.T.H. equipment. Westinghouse, however, would not accept the cancellation of the contract and the Metropolitan Railway had to take delivery of these equipments in addition, which were then taken into stock as spares.

Later in 1905 the optional order for a further 10 × 6-car trains was taken up, and this time B.T.H. equipment was specified from the onset. The type of equipment ordered was similar to that already specified for the new Hammersmith & City Joint Stock, utilizing GE76 traction motors with 150 h.p. rating. The B.T.H. Co. at this time found that it could not meet the delivery requirements for this specification, and offered 56 traction motors of GE69 type with 200 h.p. rating similar to those already provided for the District working. Together with the six spare cars there were 26 double-equipped motor cars to be fitted, and this offer enabled 14 of the cars to be fitted out in this way, leaving 12 to have the equipment originally specified. The offer was made in the form that the GE69 equipments would be rented with the option to purchase, or be replaced by GE76 equipments, after the completion of the Hammersmith & City contract. In the event, the Metropolitan purchased the GE69

[42]

38 *Interior of 1905 Third Class car*

equipments. The first B.T.H.-equipped train ran in service in April 1906.

The provision of two basically different equipments then provided an operating problem. The B.T.H. equipments differed materially from the Westinghouse or B.W.E. equipments as they were known, because the B.T.H. used electro-magnetic contactors directly energized by control wires utilizing the 600-volt supply, while the B.W.E. used low-voltage electro-pneumatic contactors. The B.W.E. system required 9 control wires while the B.T.H. system used 10. The two types of motor car could not, therefore, be connected in multiple. In addition, the two types of B.T.H. equipment, although compatible in operation using the same system of control, were not normally matched in the same train because of the uneven distribution of power.

The majority of equipments were B.W.E. providing a total of 28×6-car trains. 13×6 B.T.H. type trains could be provided, 7×6 with GE69 equipment and 6×6 with GE76, but not all these trains could be put into service at once because this total utilized all the six spare motor cars, and there were insufficient trailer cars to make up more than a total of 38×6-car trains.

The 1904 stock, which was entirely composed of B.W.E.-equipped cars, had been provided with 9-core jumper connections down both sides known as the 'Up' and 'Down' sides, enabling individual cars to be turned end-for-end. The turning of trailer cars was rarely necessary, and subsequently trailer cars were provided with the 10-core B.T.H. system on the 'Up' side and the 9-core B.W.E. system on the 'Down' side. Trailer cars so equipped could be operated in either type of train. It was subsequently appreciated that the B.T.H. 10-core, which had to be insulated for 600 volts, was the more important electrically, and could be used for low voltage without detriment if suitable cable adaptors were provided, enabling a 9-core jumper to be coupled into a 10-core socket. The B.W.E. 9-core were then not renewed when any rewiring was necessary, all repair provisions being based on the B.T.H. 10-core arrangement on trailer cars. It was not possible, of course, to use B.W.E.-equipped driving trailers as operating units for B.T.H. trains, but the provision of 10-core jumper sockets enabled them to be marshalled in block 6-car formations, with B.T.H. motor cars at the outer ends if necessary.

The motor cars had pressed steel frame bogies with a 7 ft. wheelbase, and the original cars were fitted with oak shoebeams mounted transversely across the frames. The beams placed at the outer ends of each bogie carried negative as well as positive shoes. In addition, on the inner end of one bogie a short beam carried a negative shoe. The motor cars, therefore, had four positive and three negative shoes. In addition to the control lines a positive and negative bus line was carried down the train to enable the collector shoes to be coupled together, and collector shoes were subsequently fitted to driving trailers. This shoebeam arrangement on motor cars was subsequently altered to the conventional arrangement, having the positive shoebeam mounted between the axle boxes, after difficulty had been encountered on the District section of the Circle.

Both types of trains were provided with an 8G2 type Westinghouse compressor, supplying compressed air at 60 p.s.i., which was used for the Westinghouse 'quick acting' air brake as well as traction control on B.W.E.-equipped trains. The brakes were applied on each car by means of a large single brake cylinder acting through rigging to the blocks on each wheel. In addition to the driver's brake valve, an emergency valve was provided on each car adjacent to the conductor or gateman's position. [43]

The door arrangement at the vestibules was rather elaborate. A hinged door was provided over the buffer plate and twin sliding doors between the saloon and the vestibule. The hinged door was subsequently converted to a sliding door and the twin sliding doors removed altogether. The only access to the station platforms was through single sliding doors on each side of the end vestibules. This arrangement proved to be unsatisfactory on the busy Circle service, and the Metropolitan contemplated converting the cars to compartments—compartment stock was considered much superior for quick loading and unloading. This leaning towards compartment stock was never completely eliminated from Metropolitan thinking. In 1911 work began on the provision of centre sliding doors and on altered seating arrangement. The work entailed was considerable and several different versions were produced. The seating capacity of the motor cars was generally reduced to 38 and the trailers to 48. At this time, too, these sliding doors were fitted with self-acting lock mechanisms which enabled the number of conductors carried on the trains to be reduced to two and finally to one guard.

By 1927 the traction motors on the B.W.E. trains became a maintenance liability, and converting these cars to trailer cars to operate with new motor coaches began.

The replacement of the original electric stock did not commence until 1936.

11 | Electrification of the Inner Circle

The introduction of electric traction on the Inner Circle was arranged to commence on 1 July 1905. The operation was planned on a similar basis to that which had been worked under steam traction. The Metropolitan would provide all the trains on one rail and some trains on the other because it owned the greater mileage. The Metropolitan electric service began on 1 July, but was withdrawn later on the same day. The District began its Ealing–Whitechapel service on the same day, of course serving the southern part of the Circle.

Soon after the service commenced, three 'disasters' occurred which caused traffic through the central area to be dislocated. A derailment at Acton Town and flooding at Hammersmith caused the District main line services to be seriously delayed, while a Metropolitan Circle train overturned the positive current rails in District territory, interrupting the Circle service. This latter incident was attributed to the Metropolitan type shoegear which was mounted outside the bogie frames, allowing the positive shoegear to alter its position relative to the rail on curves. This condition had not been properly taken into account on the District section of the railway, and all the Metropolitan trains had to be withdrawn and the shoegear modified. The District trains did not suffer from this malady because the positive collector shoe was

mounted on a shoebeam suspended between the axle boxes.

Until the difficulties were sorted out between the two railways the Metropolitan trains were confined to working a shuttle service from Aldgate to South Kensington on its own tracks. This shuttle service worked alongside a restored steam service until September, by which time the Metropolitan had altered the positive shoegear on the 12 trains required to maintain their part of the joint service. The Metropolitan placed two electric trains on the Outer rail on 13 September and one on the 14th. The District added two trains three days later, two more on the 19th, and one on the 20th. The full electric Inner Circle service began on 24 September. The last steam train operated on the Inner Circle service on 22 September 1905.

The traffic did not increase to the desired extent with

39 *Side view of District Railway electric locomotive. They were originally used, in pairs, to haul LNWR Outer Circle trains and, in later years, Southend through trains*

the introduction of electric traction, and the District announced that it wished to reduce its trains operating the service to 4-car formations. As the payments between the railways were adjusted on a car mile basis, the District also wished to raise additional charges for energy consumed by the 6-car Metropolitan trains on the District section on the south side of the Inner Circle between South Kensington and Aldgate. The Metropolitan, instead of agreeing to these increased charges, also reduced the train formation to four cars.

From 1907 most of the Metropolitan trains were made up with 4-car sets, having one GE69 type motor car at one end with a driving trailer at the other. The [45] balance of the Circle trains had to be made up with two motor cars of the GE76 type to give the required performance. The use of the sets with only one motor car caused some difficulty to First Class passengers, whose accommodation was also provided in the driving trailer. It was never possible, therefore, to anticipate whether the next train would be arranged with the driving trailer leading or trailing, and First Class passengers were seriously inconvenienced. Some further difficulties in the provision of the Circle service arose and eventually, after considerable negotiations, the Metropolitan took over the entire weekday working of the Inner Circle service from 4 November 1907. This strained the electric rolling stock position of the Metropolitan which, in turn, gave impetus to the conversion of surplus steam stock to

40 *Coupling end of electric locomotive showing both link coupling and Ward coupling*

electric working.

The District, on the other hand, now had surplus rolling stock. Arrangements were subsequently made to introduce the Putney Bridge–Edgware Road service. The introduction of this service did not completely equate the mileage requirements between the two railways, and this was adjusted by operating some District trains on the Inner Circle service, especially on Sundays, a practice which persisted for many years. District trains were withdrawn from Inner Circle service completely on 1 November 1926, except for three trains worked on Sundays to enable a nucleus of District crews to be kept familiar with the road.

At the time of the electrification there were two 'foreign' railway services on the Circle tracks; the southern half of the Outer Circle provided by the London & North Western Railway on the District section, and the through suburban trains to the city provided from Paddington by the Great Western Railway on the Metropolitan section.

The Outer Circle service began in 1872 from Broad Street by way of Willesden Junction and Addison Road (now Olympia) to Earl's Court and then over the District tracks to Mansion House. This service was worked entirely by the London & North Western Railway with its own rolling stock and locomotives. To avoid the retention of steam engines on this service the District arranged to provide electric locomotives for hauling the London & North Western trains between Earl's Court and Mansion House. The steam locomotives continued to operate this service until 4 December 1905 when the electric locomotives took over, engines being changed at Earl's Court.

For this duty the Metropolitan Amalgamated Railway Carriage & Wagon Co. built 10 electric locomotives which normally worked in pairs. These vehicles, built of steel, weighed 28 tons and had box-like bodies just over 25 feet long to house the traction control equipment. Each locomotive was provided with two sets of traction control equipment which controlled four GE69 type traction motors, each pair being separately operated in series/parallel by the multiple unit control.

On 1 January 1909 the Outer Circle service was cut back to Earl's Court, as the District wanted the train paths for its own services which had been increased when the track improvements were completed west of Hammersmith. The District locomotives were then rendered redundant and three were scrapped in 1911. For a short time some trains were made up with one of these locomotives at each end of a rake of four trailer cars. However, negotiations had been completed with the London, Tilbury & Southend Railway for a through train service to be operated from the western suburb of Ealing to Southend. The Tilbury line provided two special trains sets to operate this through service, the trains being hauled between Barking and Ealing Broadway by the District locomotives again coupled in pairs. There were now three pairs with one locomotive spare. The through Southend service lasted from 1 June 1910 until 30 September 1939, after the outbreak of the Second World War.

The locomotives were renovated in 1922 when the GE69 equipments, including the traction motors, were replaced by GE260 type surplus from the 'F' stock. This reconditioning work was one of the first such jobs undertaken in the newly constructed Acton Works.

To enable the through suburban services of the Great Western to continue operating from Paddington to the City the Metropolitan also provided some locomotives from the same builders, but these locomotives were

41 *Interior of District electric locomotive, looking towards a driving end*

required for other duties and their more complicated story requires separate treatment.

The last steam-hauled passenger service through Baker Street on the Circle section was operated on 31 December 1906, when the through Richmond service worked by the Great Western was cut back to Notting Hill (now Ladbroke Grove). On 1 January 1907 electric locomotives began hauling through Great Western trains from Bishop's Road to Aldgate and this type of working continued until the Second World War caused withdrawal of the arrangement on 16 September 1939.

Neither of these through workings was restored, although Metropolitan locomotives continued to haul 'steam' stock from Liverpool Street over the north side of the Circle on the Metropolitan country services until September 1961.

12 | The Hammersmith & City Line

In 1861 the Hammersmith & City Railway was incorporated as an independent venture to act as a feeder to the Metropolitan Railway, and made working arrangements with both the Metropolitan and Great Western Railways. It was vested in the two companies jointly on 1 July 1867. The line was constructed of mixed gauge joining the Great Western tracks about a mile west of Paddington. Initially the Great Western supplied broad gauge rolling stock and motive power, beginning a service between Hammersmith and Farringdon Street on 13 June 1864, just 17 months after the Metropolitan Railway itself became revenue earning. The Metropolitan Railway took over the Hammersmith to Farringdon workings with

[48]

standard gauge trains on 1 April 1865. Meanwhile a branch from the Hammersmith line to the West London line had been built, with the junction at Latimer Road station to enable trains to operate to Kensington (Addison Road). The Great Western began working trains over this route which, on 1 August 1872, became the Middle Circle service. The trains then operated from Moorgate to Paddington, proceeding over the Hammersmith & City tracks to Latimer Road and so, by way of this new connection, to Kensington (Addison Road) and on to a junction with the District which enabled through trains to continue to Earl's Court and Mansion House. On 30 June 1900 this service was curtailed at Earl's Court, but it was still operated by Great Western trains. On 1 February 1905, however, the service was taken over by the Metropolitan and ran between Aldgate and Addison Road only. From 3 December 1906 the service was operated entirely by electric rolling stock, but on 31 October 1910 was reduced to a shuttle from Edgware Road to Addison Road. This service ceased to operate on 21 October 1940 when the junction at Latimer Road with the West London Line received

42 *A 6-car Hammersmith & City stock electric train as originally built, in the long shed at Hammersmith Depot (A.E.I.)*

severe damage in an air raid, and was not considered worth reinstating under war-time conditions. The service was never resumed, and this connecting link was subsequently removed.

A junction was built at Grove Road, Hammersmith, with the London & South Western Railway's connection to the West London line which had been opened to traffic on 1 January 1869. The Metropolitan Railway began to run trains through from Moorgate to Richmond by way of Grove Road junction and Turnham Green on 1 October 1877. The District had begun working to Richmond on 1 June 1877. One half of the Metropolitan service was taken over by the G.W.R. on 1 January 1894, but after the electrification of the Metropolitan it was cut back to Notting Hill (which became Ladbroke Grove on 1 June 1919) and a half-hourly service was maintained until 31 December 1910. Trains on the Richmond service are said to have been the last steam-hauled passenger trains through Baker Street station, ceasing to operate on this section from 31 December 1906. In any event, during November and early December 1906, the Hammersmith & City Railway services were changed over completely to electric traction—5 November 1906 is the official date for the commencement of electric traction on the line. The District Railway did not encourage the electrification of the Grove Road connection, which would have allowed Hammersmith & City trains to run to Richmond, by impressing the London & South Western Railway it could take up all the possible timetable paths available on the two tracks between Hammersmith and Turnham Green.

Trains from Hammersmith ran over the northern section of the Inner Circle, being extended over the East London Railway to New Cross from 6 October 1884. But after electrification, which did not include the East London Railway, this service ceased on 2 December 1906, and the trains were diverted to Whitechapel. After 31 March 1913, when the East London Line was electrified, a through service began again which lasted until 20 November 1939, when the East London once more reverted to shuttle workings.

Until 1878, when the fly-under east of Westbourne Park was completed, the H. & C. trains had to cross the Great Western tracks on the level to reach Bishop's Road where the junction with the Metropolitan was made. This arrangement caused interference with main line operations and the segregation of tracks became necessary.

The steam-hauled rolling stock used on the Hammersmith & City Railway was supplied by either the Metropolitan or the Great Western. After 1867 the railway was managed by a Joint Committee of the two companies and powers were obtained in 1902 for electrification.

The Great Western built a power station at Park Royal and maintained and operated the substations. There were substations at Royal Oak and Shepherd's Bush, and these were equipped with La Cour type converters, a system different from any other traction substation then being installed in London. The La Cour converter consisted of two machines which were coupled together like a motor generator set, but also coupled electrically in a circuit known as cascade. It was unlike the normal rotary converter of the era which had one rotating armature with AC fed at one end and DC collected from the commutator at the other end. This system of converting an AC supply to DC was not used elsewhere on London's Underground. The new electric rolling stock was operated in the name of the Joint Railway, but some vehicles were the property of the Great Western and others the Metropolitan. The Metropolitan, however, maintained all the vehicles and operated the running

[49]

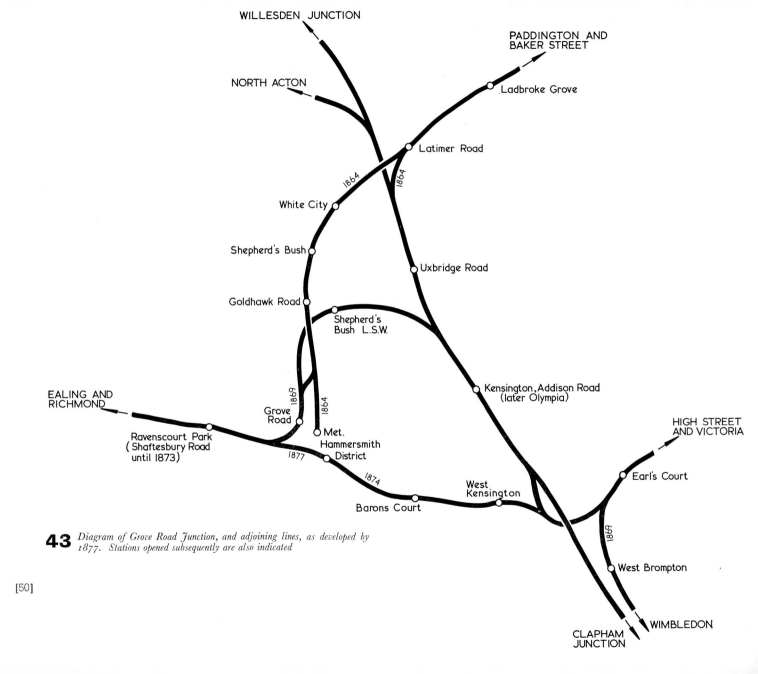

WILLESDEN JUNCTION

PADDINGTON AND
BAKER STREET

NORTH ACTON

Ladbroke Grove

Latimer Road

1864

1864

White City

Shepherd's Bush

Uxbridge Road

Goldhawk Road

Shepherd's
Bush L.S.W.

1869

1864

EALING AND
RICHMOND

Grove
Road

Met.
Hammersmith
District

Kensington, Addison Road
(later Olympia)

Ravenscourt Park
(Shaftesbury Road
until 1873)

1877

1874

HIGH STREET
AND VICTORIA

Earl's Court

West
Kensington

Barons Court

1869

West Brompton

43 *Diagram of Grove Road Junction, and adjoining lines, as developed by*
1877. Stations opened subsequently are also indicated

CLAPHAM
JUNCTION

WIMBLEDON

shed. When the stock was replaced in 1936, the new stock was owned entirely by London Transport, but the tracks and substations were not vested in London Transport until nationalization on 1 January 1948.

The rolling stock required for the Hammersmith & City electrification and the through service to Whitechapel consisted of 20 × 6-car trains. After the extension of the services to the East London line this total proved inadequate, and some Metropolitan rolling stock with similar traction equipments was transferred to the H. & C. fleet.

The order for the rolling stock was placed with the Metropolitan Amalgamated Railway Carriage & Wagon Co. and was provided in 3-car sets usually operated in 6-car formations M–T–CT–CT–T–M. The control or driving trailer cars were First Class, following the Metropolitan practice. The cars were all of the open saloon type and the motor cars were at first provided with small luggage compartments. The vehicles were just over 52 ft. long and 8 ft. 9 in. wide.

The traction control equipment provided was BTH GE76 type, each motor car being provided with two sets of equipment and four 150 h.p. traction motors. The cars, finished in Metropolitan style, were varnished teak with the cant rail and waist rail in white, but in addition to a monogram with H. & C. on the side panels they originally had 'Great Western and Metropolitan' on the upper panels. It is understood that originally those vehicles owned by each railway had the owning railway's name written first. First Class accommodation on these trains was withdrawn on 4 May 1936, when the peak-hour service was extended to Barking and some additional new rolling stock of District type was provided to augment the fleet. The 20 × 6-car trains had been increased by a further 4 × 6-car trains of Metropolitan 150 GE76 type by 1930, and these remained part of the H. & C. fleet until withdrawn for disposal. Due to war conditions arising in 1938/39 many of these trains were stored or converted for other purposes. In fact 4 × 6-car trains, of which 18 cars out of the 24 came from the original H. & C. stock, were lent to the Mersey Railway from 1942 until 1945 to provide an emergency reserve for maintaining the vital link under the Mersey in war conditions.

13 | The East London Line

In 1818 Marc Isambard Brunel patented a tunnelling shield and joined a consortium which formed a new company, the Thames Tunnel Company, to build a tunnel under the Thames between Wapping and Rotherhithe.

Brunel's tunnelling shield was the first of its kind in the world, and the development of this device has made possible the building of all London's Tube railways. The building of the first tunnel by this means, however, was an epic of endurance and perseverance, a story which has been told many times, but for the purpose of this history it suffices to record that it was completed and brought into full use as a pedestrian subway on 25 March 1843.

In 1865 this tunnel was acquired by the East London

44 *Reconditioned 'C' stock leading a southbound East London Line train at Rotherhithe about 1950*

Railway. Trains first ran through the tunnel in 1869, when a service from New Cross (this station was renamed New Cross Gate in 1923) to Wapping was begun on 7 December by the London, Brighton & South Coast Railway. On 10 April 1876 the line was extended northwards from Wapping to Shoreditch, where a junction was made with the Great Eastern Railway enabling the trains to be run into the Liverpool Street terminal of that railway from south London. The LBSC ran trains from East Croydon, and for eight years from 1876 trains ran between Brighton and Liverpool Street over this route.

There were six intermediate stations, at Deptford Road (renamed Surrey Docks in 1911), Rotherhithe, Wapping, Shadwell, Whitechapel, and Shoreditch. The line was double throughout except at New Cross where only a single platform was provided. The spur to the New Cross station of the South Eastern Railway was opened to traffic on 1 April 1880, and this railway ran trains into Liverpool Street from Addiscombe Road.

On 3 March 1884 St. Mary's junction with the District Railway just west of Whitechapel was opened, and the management of the railway was taken over jointly by five railways, including the Metropolitan and the District. On 6 October 1884, Metropolitan steam trains began to work to the New Cross station of the South Eastern Railway, and the District to the New Cross station of the London, Brighton & South Coast Railway. This latter station was renamed New Cross Gate in 1923, after the formation of the Southern Railway.

Following the electrification of the Circle in 1905 the through District service was withdrawn, as the East London Railway was not at that time included in the electrification scheme, but, as previously mentioned, steam trains from the Hammersmith & City Line continued until 2 December 1906. Steam passenger services, however, were continued by the two southern railways—the LBSC to Shoreditch and the S.E.R. to Whitechapel.

The East London Railway decided that the shuttle steam services were unsatisfactory and wanted to provide through services to the City again, so a decision was made to electrify the line. Part of the agreement on the electrification scheme provided for the District to supply the power from Lots Road Power Station and for the Metropolitan to supply the train service. The East London Railway in fact never owned any rolling stock.

The service, after the introduction of electric traction on 31 March 1913, consisted of a number of 4-car trains of Metropolitan open saloon stock from South Kensington round the Metropolitan side of the Circle to New Cross, and 2-car shuttle trains operating from Shoreditch. To provide the appropriate accommodation in the 2-car shuttles the Metropolitan converted a number of the First Class driving trailers into composite vehicles. In 1914 the Metropolitan South Kensington trains were withdrawn and the Hammersmith & City service was diverted from Whitechapel to New Cross in their place.

In 1921 the Metropolitan Railway took over management but in 1925 freehold of the East London Railway was acquired by the Southern Railway (subject, of course, to the 1884 lease). In recognition of this the Metropolitan type nameplates used on the stations were changed from a red lozenge behind the name to a diamond coloured green. After the formation of London Transport in 1933 the line continued to be owned by the Southern Railway. The passenger service continued to be provided by Hammersmith & City rolling stock until these trains ran through to Barking or were terminated at Whitechapel. A rush-hour service from Hammersmith to East Ham was operated from 30 March 1936, and through to Barking

from 4 May. At the same time one-class travel was introduced on the Hammersmith & City line. Subsequently the East London service reverted to a shuttle from Whitechapel and Shoreditch.

After nationalization in 1948 the line passed to the control of London Transport completely. Subsequently goods service on the line ceased, allowing the junction with the main line at Shoreditch to be removed.

The trains initially transferred for shuttle duty on the line were 4-car sets of District Line hand-worked door stock, which were eventually designated 'H' class, and the general rolling stock maintenance was transferred from Neasden to Ealing Common. However, one unit used on the service was still maintained by Neasden and was of considerable interest, being a 3-car set containing the two experimental motor cars having the prototype equipment for the 'T' stock together with the Wembley Exhibition trailer car. This train set continued to work on the East London Line until scrapped.

The transfer of the 'F' stock to the Metropolitan began in 1950 and by 1953 the East London service had been taken over by 4-car sets of this stock. These sets had to be adapted by the provision of 'loudaphones' in the single-equipped motor cars, because through communication of this kind was not previously provided in the driving cars normally placed in the middle of an 8-car train. About 8×4 units were arranged for working the East London service although only six, including spares, were required to be allocated to the line at one time. The 'F' stock was withdrawn from the East London Line in September 1963 when 4-car 'Q' stock began working the service.

This type of stock will continue to provide the service on the line for another decade as 5×4-car sets have been specially rehabilitated to maintain the service when all the rest of the 'Q' stock has been withdrawn.

[53]

14 | The Whitechapel & Bow Line

Incorporated in 1897, the Whitechapel & Bow Railway was constructed to join the District from Whitechapel to the London Tilbury & Southend Railway at Campbell Road junction. The line was controlled jointly by the two companies, and was opened on 2 June 1902. Trains then ran through from the District Line over the Tilbury tracks as far as East Ham, and some ran on to Upminster.

The two railway companies bought an equal number of new train sets similar to those already operating on the District to provide the additional service. These trains were known as 'Joint Stock' and normally worked the through service. The Tilbury company fitted at least two locomotives with condensing apparatus to work

through the tunnels to Whitechapel. Locomotive changing normally took place at Whitechapel but some District locomotives worked through at least to East Ham.

The projection of the District trains through to East Ham overloaded the existing tracks of the Tilbury line beyond Campbell Road junction, and powers were obtained to widen the lines by two extra tracks. These powers included electrification in order that the through connection as far as East Ham from the District would continue after completion of the main electrification scheme.

Electric trains began running to East Ham on 20 August 1905, and the through steam service to Upminster from Whitechapel ceased on 30 September 1905. The electrified trackage was extended to Barking and the through service to this point began on 1 April 1908.

The Tilbury company arranged to purchase from the

45 *Southend through train leaving Ealing Broadway composed of Tilbury-type rolling stock about 1927*

[54]

46 *An earlier photograph before the locomotives were modified at Acton Works. This train is also composed of Tilbury rolling stock*

District Railway a number of cars to provide the service to East Ham and Barking. A total of 37 motor cars and 37 trailer cars was transferred initially to the Tilbury Company for a sum of £130,000. The cars continued to be maintained and were interchangeable with District-owned cars. They were at first painted in a distinctive green livery, but this difference was not maintained for very long as the cars were repainted the same as the District, and were completely absorbed in the fleet, not necessarily working on the Barking service or even beyond Whitechapel. This ownership of a number of District Line cars by the Tilbury Railway and its successor, the London Midland & Scottish Railway, continued until

nationalization when the necessity for this special book-keeping became unnecessary. The actual LMS owner-ship at nationalization amounted to 57 motor cars and 53 trailer cars.

The 7¾-mile extension of the track quadrupling from Barking to Upminster and the electrification of the two additional tracks came into operation on 12 September 1932, when the District electric trains began running beyond Barking.

Upon nationalization, on 1 January 1948, the White-chapel & Bow Railway was vested in London Transport, but the lines beyond Campbell Road junction remained the property of the British Railways Board until 1969, when the two additional tracks as far as Upminster became the property of London Transport with the

47 *Upminster Depot from the lighting tower at night. A number of mixed 'Q' stock trains are on the right*

exception of Barking and Upminster stations.

Another interesting rolling stock arrangement concerning the Tilbury line was the provision of the through Southend trains from Ealing Broadway. The Tilbury company provided, in 1912, two train sets of special saloon coaches with sliding end doors and central gangways for this service. These trains were provided with lavatories which were only fitted to the Third Class brake carriages. The lavatories were, in fact, flushing-water closets provided with sewage storage tanks which had drain valves for connection to disposal drains. In spite of this hygienic arrangement to prevent the general transfer of sewage to the tracks, the lavatories were locked while the train passed through the central area of the District line.

The trains were hauled west of Barking by District electric locomotives coupled in pairs which had been

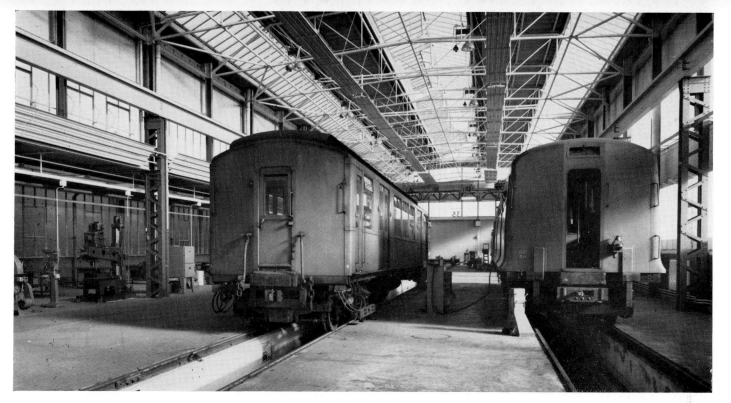

rendered surplus to requirements on the curtailment of the Outer Circle service. This service began on 1 June 1910, but until the special rolling stock was available Tilbury carriages were used. This service was withdrawn on 1 October 1939 and not reinstated. Due to war conditions the special coaches were not immediately scrapped, but were found other work for a time.

After the extension of the line to Barking a running shed for the District electric rolling stock was leased between East Ham and Barking. Following the extension to Upminster, and the increase in the service at the eastern end of the line, this accommodation proved inadequate

48 *Inside the lifting shop at Upminster. The car on the right is an R49 No. 5 car, a non-driving motor car with auto coupler. The car on the left is a Q27 after conversion from 'K' class. The A ends of the vehicles are facing the camera*

for the additional trains required. London Transport constructed in 1958 a new depot at Upminster to replace the East Ham depot. This depot included a number of new features not previously provided in an Underground Rolling Stock depot. All trains could be washed as they came out of service as twin washing machines were provided on the entry roads to the depot. The depot movements were also controlled from a control tower with power-operated points for which ground shunters were not required.

15 The Great Northern & City Line

A company with the title of the Great Northern & City Railway was formed in 1892 to build a tube railway from Finsbury Park (Great Northern Railway station) to the City. The tunnels were bored in a circular form and lined with cast iron segments in the conventional manner adopted for the tube railways, but were constructed large enough to take full-sized main-line rolling stock. The tunnels were of a diameter of 16 feet instead of the 11 ft. 8¼ in. used for most orthodox tube lines. When the line was built it was planned that eventually some physical connection would be made with the Great Northern Railway allowing through services. Even today such a connecting service is still being considered, but has not yet been achieved.

The whole line was only 3½ miles long, and from the outset electric traction was proposed. The B.T.H. Company was awarded the contract in 1901 for the whole

49 *Interior of Brush-built trailer car*

of the electrification work, which included the provision of the rolling stock, 11 trains of 7-car length and three spare motor cars being ordered.

The Sprague-Thomson-Houston 'train-control' system was specified. This was a pioneer decision as far as England was concerned, since this type of equipment had only just passed beyond the experimental stage in America. Although the Central London Railway had the honour to have been the first to operate multiple unit trains in Europe, the Great Northern & City made the decision to use such equipment some time earlier. But since passenger service on the line did not begin until 14 February 1904 the railway could not claim that it had the pioneer installation of this equipment.

The electrification controversy between the District and the Metropolitan, which was public property during the construction of the Great Northern & City, highlighted the difficulty of a tube railway in limiting the voltage drop in the running rails to 7 volts. In addition, the Great Northern & City Railway installed the first track circuit automatic signalling arrangement, and felt it desirable to keep the running rails clear of traction current interference. These two factors undoubtedly influenced the adoption of the unique collection system by the Great Northern & City Railway.

A positive and a negative current rail were used, but both were placed outside the running rails, one on either side, positioned 10 inches from the gauge line with the contact surface 2 inches above the running rail. This collection system, although unique, was of course similar to that adopted for the joint trial running of the Metropolitan and District Railways at Earl's Court some years earlier. The original arrangement continued in service until close of traffic on Saturday, 13 May 1939, when the track system was re-arranged and the rolling stock replaced with trains of pre-1938 Tube Stock from the Northern Line. The new service began on Monday, 15 May 1939, using the standard Underground four-rail system with the return rail in the centre of the track.

The line was designed from the beginning for the operation of a maximum train length of seven cars, the platform lengths being 420 feet.

The original order for rolling stock seems to have been for 77 cars to provide 11 trains of 7-car formation containing three motor cars together with three motor cars as spares. However, this order must have been modified because only 76 cars were built and of these only 32 were motor cars. Trains of 7-car length were not, in fact, operated, the maximum train formation being six cars which were uncoupled to form 2-car trains for slack hour workings.

The carbodies were built by two contractors, the Brush Electrical Engineering Co. Ltd. of Loughborough and the Electric Railway Tramway & Carriage Works of Preston, and were of two basic types. The majority of the cars were of all teak construction and were referred to as 'wooden' cars. The last eighteen, consisting of six motor cars and twelve trailer cars, were constructed by Brush in 1906, with steel panels and framework, being referred to as 'steel' cars.

On the motor cars the electrical equipment, which was of the electro-magnetic contactor type on the Sprague–Thomson–Houston system controlling two GE66 type traction motors, was housed in a fireproofed compartment behind the driving cab.

The control system connected the two traction motors under hand-notching of the master controller on each motor car in series/parallel with open circuit transition. Until 1906 the controllers were not provided with a dead man's handle, and assistant motormen were carried.

This practice continued for some years on full-length trains after this date, although the 2-car portions carried one motorman after the fitting of this safety equipment.

The motor cars were provided with two motor bogies, each carrying only one traction motor. This design, constructed in England to the requirements of the McGuire Manufacturing Co. of Chicago, was unique in Underground practice at the time. The single-motor bogie did not re-appear again until 1935, when it was fitted to the Experimental Streamlined Tube rolling stock.

The trailer bogies, constructed by the Brush Company, were its standard type 'E' design having cast steel side frames, a swing bolster and inside brake blocks.

The air brake originally fitted to the G.N. & City stock was on the Christensen system, which employed a tripcock device installed on the roof of the motor cars. This worked in connection with an automatic signalling system devised originally by J. E. Spagnoletti.

The multiple unit control line passed down the centre of the roofs of the cars, the jumper couplings being located in this position. There were no through bus lines, however, and each motor car picked up its own current supply by means of four collector shoes, two on the outside of each bogie.

Power was originally supplied from the railway's own power station at Poole Street, Islington, but after control had been acquired by the Metropolitan Railway this was closed down and the power obtained from Neasden Generating Station. This old Great Northern & City power station became the Gainsborough Film Studios.

The cars were coupled by link couplers with centre buffers, an arrangement peculiar to the G.N. & City. The intermediate ends of all cars were fitted with gates which until the withdrawal of this stock in May 1939 [59]

50/51 *Brush-built steel cars*

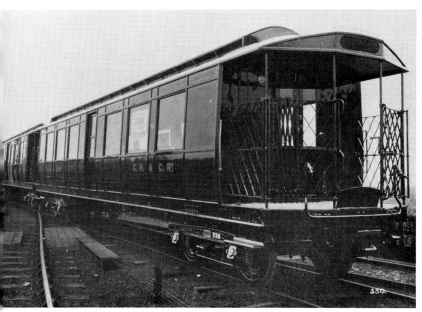

required manual operation by gatemen.

Sliding doors were provided in the centre of the cars, but these were only used at the terminal stations as they could not be opened from inside the cars. Special porters were employed to operate these doors at Moorgate station to speed up the unloading arrangements. The conductors or gatemen on the trains worked the hand-operated spring-locking gates on the end platforms. To start the train the conductor at the rear rang a bell to the conductor next in line. The foremost conductor gave the starting signal for the driver to start the train.

The seats in the carbodies were transverse in the American fashion; the 'wooden' trailer cars seated 58 and the 'steel' trailers 64. The motor cars of each type seated four less. The body length was 40 ft. 8 in. while the overall length over the buffers, including the platforms, was 50 ft. 6 in. The bogie wheelbase was over 6 feet and the bogie centres were 34 ft. 6 in. apart.

Each car was illuminated by 15 lamps of 16 candle power. Originally some of the cars were provided inside with an illuminated indicator which gave the name of the next station; this equipment was not satisfactory and was subsequently removed.

The railway was not a financial success probably because the capital outlay to build 16 ft. diameter tunnels was excessive for a line which was very short in length. The Metropolitan Railway acquired the assets on 30 June 1913.

The Great Northern & City Railway obtained in 1905, from the Metropolitan Amalgamated Railway Carriage & Wagon Co., a double-bogie locomotive similar in appearance to the vehicles built at the same time for the Metropolitan Railway. The vehicle was provided with four GE66 traction motors and the appropriate control equipment; when the Metropolitan Railway acquired

52 *Wooden motor car*

control, this locomotive was numbered 21 in the fleet. On the formation of the London Passenger Transport Board it was renumbered L33—it was finally scrapped on 4 March 1948 after it had been converted to the conventional fourth rail system to enable the stock transfer movements to be completed.

This locomotive was used to transfer rolling stock into and out of Drayton Park depot which, in addition to its isolation by having a unique electrical track system, had no road access. Stores and heavy material required had to be transferred by railway wagon.

The transfer of the passenger rolling stock to Neasden Works also began in this way, but from the goods yard a main line steam locomotive transferred the vehicles to the Metropolitan Widened Lines at Aldersgate, where a Metropolitan locomotive took over. The dimensions of the Great Northern & City cars, however, were such that they could not negotiate the Finchley Road tunnels and they had, therefore, to be transferred by way of High Street (Kensington) and Rayners Lane. The District provided a pilotman from High Street to Rayners Lane, where a further reversal was necessary before transfer to Neasden could be completed. This procedure continued until the original rolling stock was replaced, as the Great Northern & City cars never received an overhaul at Acton Works.

When the service was first begun only one class of travel was provided, which was normally accepted practice of a 'tube' type railway. However, soon after the Metropolitan obtained control, First Class accommodation was provided and the carriage of parcels on the trains was introduced.

In 1930, in order to improve the service on the line, the Metropolitan transferred six Metropolitan BWE150 type motor cars, each with four traction motors, to the line. These cars, together with some existing trailer cars, provided three additional trains but allowed all the other trains of 6-car length to be equipped with three motor cars. The service interval was then reduced to $2\frac{1}{2}$ minutes at the peak. Because of the limited stabling accommodation at Drayton Park, however, the introduction of these six additional vehicles required the withdrawal of six trailer cars from the fleet which were subsequently scrapped at Neasden.

When First Class accommodation was provided on 15 February 1915 one trailer car of each train set was modified to give 28 seats smoking and 26 seats non-smoking, for the privileged class. This facility was withdrawn on 25 March 1934 after the formation of the London Passenger Transport Board. When tube rolling stock from the Northern Line took over the working on 15 May 1939 the original vehicles were scrapped.

Finsbury Park station was required subsequently for the new Victoria Line to provide an interchange with the Piccadilly Line, and the Northern City was then cut back to operate from Drayton Park to Moorgate. While the construction work was being undertaken for the Victoria Line, a bus service was provided connecting Drayton Park with Finsbury Park, and the facilities to the passengers were reduced. However, with the opening of the Victoria Line, a new same-level interchange at Highbury has helped to restore to the line, now known as the Highbury Branch of the Northern Line, some of its former traffic.

[62]

53 *An Aveling & Porter engine with a Brill mixed train. Date unknown*

16 | The Brill Branch

A section of the Metropolitan that could be described as an 'appendage' was the Oxford & Aylesbury Tramroad, known to most Metropolitan employees as the Brill Branch. In its earlier days it was called the Wotton Tramway.

It was originally constructed by the Duke of Buckingham to connect Quainton Road station with his estate at Wotton and was opened for private traffic by horse traction on 1 April 1871. It was subsequently extended to Brill, but it was not originally intended for public passenger use, being confined to persons accompanying cattle or merchandise, or estate workmen; local pressure, however, caused the Duke to obtain a passenger carriage which was duly placed in public service in January 1872, at the same time as the first locomotive appeared.

This locomotive, built by Aveling & Porter of Rochester, was a single cylinder engine and owed its design characteristics more to steam road rollers or traction engines. The drive was by means of a toothed sprocket on the crankshaft driving a chain which was connected to the two pairs of driving wheels. A similar engine was obtained later in the same year. One of these locomotives was subsequently found working in a brickworks by the Industrial Locomotive Society: it was reconstructed and may now be seen in its original colours in the Museum of British Transport.

[63]

54 *The preserved engine in the Transport Museum*

55 *Locomotive 23 bursts out of a copse to reach Wood Siding station, Brill branch. A view taken from the station which shows the extremely wooded countryside through which the railway ran. At Wood Siding the 'Met' line crossed the Great Western main line, and the iron bridge which it used was one of the few points at which the Brill branch track could, in later years, be traced*

56 *Locomotive 23 on Neasden turntable after restoration to 1903 condition for preservation in the Transport Museum*

In 1883 a scheme was promoted to link Oxford with Quainton Road by a railway but these proposals fell through and subsequently a modified proposal, known as the Oxford & Aylesbury Tramroad, came into being with the intention of extending the Wotton Tramway to Oxford.

In 1894 this concern took over the working of the Wotton Tramway and a small amount of rolling stock was acquired for the purpose. Two locomotives built by Manning, Wardle & Co. of Leeds were acquired, No. 1 named *Huddersfield* (obviously secondhand as it was built in 1876) and No. 2, built new in 1894 named *Brill*. *Huddersfield* was subsequently withdrawn and a third similar locomotive built in 1899 named *Wotton* appeared. These locomotives were 0–6–0 saddle tanks with inside 12 in. diameter cylinders. The driving wheels were only 3 feet in diameter and the locomotives weighed about 18 tons in working order. One of these locomotives subsequently ended its career as a contractor's engine on the construction of the Great West Road about 1929.

On 1 December 1899 the Metropolitan Railway took over the working of the line but never acquired the Oxford & Aylesbury Tramroad. Subsequently, on 2 April 1906, the Metropolitan & Great Central Joint Committee assumed control of the operations and this body remained in being until nationalization, the London Passenger Transport Board taking over the Metropolitan functions on this joint committee. It was in the name of the Metropolitan & Great Central Joint Committee that all traffic ceased on the Brill Branch on 30 November 1935.

The Metropolitan transferred two 'A' class locomotives, Nos. 23 and 41, to take over the duties but it was strictly only one engine in steam. Each engine performed a week's work on the Brill Line. The duty engine took up its duty

57 *General view of Quainton Road station, junction of the Brill branch and Verney Junction lines, 1935. Locomotive 41, the other Brill branch engine, is bustling on the branch lines with a mixed train*

58 *Wotton station, on the last summer of operation. Locomotive 41, working bunker first, with a rigid 8-wheeled coach that often ran in a mixed train with coal trucks. The guard proudly displays his 'Met' cap. Siding, right foreground*

roster on Monday morning and returned to Neasden on the following Sunday. Locomotive 23 has survived and has been preserved in honourable retirement in the Transport Museum. The Metropolitan also retained for use on the line five coaches of 1866 vintage built by the Oldbury Carriage Company, consisting of one First Class, one Brake Van, and three Third Class coaches, although the service train complement often only contained one passenger coach. Unfortunately none of these coaches, which were examples of the original Metropolitan Railway rolling stock, was retained after the line closed down.

There were four level crossings, the gates being opened by the train staff themselves. The train was required to cross these level crossings at 2 m.p.h.!

17 | Expansion of the Branch

The first Underground branch line was the separately promoted Metropolitan & St. John's Wood Railway. This line was opened to traffic as far as Swiss Cottage on 13 April 1868, but was only single track with passing

places at the two intermediate stations, St. John's Wood Road and Marlborough Road. A connection with the Metropolitan was provided at Baker Street.

The gradient of the line was steep and five powerful 0–6–0 tank locomotives were built by the Worcester Engine Co. for the service which ran through from Moorgate. The Metropolitan, however, required the paths on the main line section for other services. Through passenger operation over the Baker Street junction was, therefore, withdrawn on 8 March 1869 and not revived until 28 January 1907 after electrification. The original engines were actually too powerful and far too extravagant in fuel consumption so that, after a very short period in

59 *Neasden Works and Power Station after the electrification and the four-tracking to Wembley Park, looking from the north*

service in London, they were sold to railways in South Wales where their characteristics were of more value.

An extension was opened on 30 June 1879 as far as West Hampstead with an intermediate station at Finchley Road, but the St. John's Wood section from Baker Street was not completely doubled until 10 July 1882, when a separate tunnel was constructed alongside the old single line tunnel.

When the line reached Harrow on 2 August 1880, the district through which it ran was rural. There was no intermediate station between Neasden and Harrow. Wembley Park was not opened until 1894, Preston Road Halt (south of the road bridge, not the present station) in 1908, and Northwick Park as late as 1923. This station was also rebuilt, in 1931, as the present island platform.

The first sign of 'expansion' rather than 'extension' was the construction of double tracks alongside the original tracks from Harrow to Canfield Place near Finchley Road. These tracks were leased to the Great Central Railway to enable it to gain access to its new London terminal at Marylebone. The agreement with the Metropolitan included the undertaking that no station would be constructed south of the River Brent, so that no platforms were installed on these tracks except [67]

60 *Neasden Depot about 1950, from the south end with the Power Station in the background*

an emergency wartime arrangement at Neasden in 1940. These tracks are now used exclusively for the diesel train service to Marylebone. Passenger service over the tracks into Marylebone began on 15 March 1899.

The tracks were laid in two distinct sections. The first from Finchley Road to Wembley Park, completed by July 1898, was used by Metropolitan trains for a time to enable alterations to be made to the original Metropolitan tracks. Access to these two tracks was provided south of Preston Road and this junction was used by Great Central trains until 31 March 1901, when the additional two tracks to Harrow were completed. Harrow station itself was not four-tracked until 1908.

With the opening of the Uxbridge branch from Harrow on 4 July 1904 the Metropolitan became congested, particularly affecting those services operating into the country, and arrangements were made to construct two additional tracks on the north or 'Up' side of the original tracks between Finchley Road and Wembley Park. The first section between Finchley Road and Kilburn was brought into use on 30 November 1913. Further four-tracking arrangements as far as Wembley Park began operating in January 1914, with additional platforms at Willesden Green, Neasden, and Wembley Park, but not at Dollis Hill, Kilburn, or West Hampstead. Quadrupling of all sections to Wembley Park was completed by 31 May 1915. The provision of these tracks enabled fast trains to be worked, which were only impeded by the Finchley Road to Baker Street bottleneck. By careful timetabling, the effect of this was reduced.

The passing of the 1929 Development Act enabled the Metropolitan to acquire capital to begin two important projects: (i) the construction of the Stanmore branch from Wembley Park, (ii) the extension of the four-tracking north of Wembley Park to Harrow-on-the-Hill. The four-tracking to Harrow came into full use on 10 January 1932. The actual re-arrangement of the tracks was complicated. The two additional new tracks were laid on the north or 'Up' side, but for some reason which is obscure it was decided to build new stations at Preston Road and Northwick Park, with platforms having access to these tracks and to use the two older tracks for through fast trains.

This orientation of the tracks was unfortunate, as it produced two operating difficulties: fast trains had to cross the slow or stopping trains at Wembley Park; and Stanmore trains, when this branch was opened on 10 December 1932, had to cross the fast tracks to reach the branch. The burrowing junction for the Stanmore line was not constructed until 1938, when further track re-arrangements were made.

The Metropolitan realised that some relief to the bottleneck between Finchley Road and Baker Street was required, especially as these two tracks carried the country service of the railway as well as catering for a local service calling at Swiss Cottage, Marlborough Road, and St. John's Wood. Plans were prepared for a connection from a point near Kilburn & Brondesbury to Edgware Road, in a 15 ft. 6 in. tube, so that a junction to the Circle Line would be made in the same direction as that arranged at Baker Street.

In anticipation of this connection Edgware Road station was rebuilt in 1926 with four platforms as existing today, utilizing the space which had been vacated by moving the old Metropolitan Railway engine sheds to Neasden. The train destination indicators placed on the new platforms for many years contained descriptions such as 'Aylesbury Line' which were never required, because the connection to Edgware Road was never built. The congestion in the bottleneck, however, grew so that the number of stopping trains between Finchley Road and Baker Street was severely limited and subsequently stops were not, in fact, made during the peak periods.

Relief came under the 1935/40 New Works Programme by extending the Bakerloo tube to Finchley Road and re-arranging the tracks so that the Metropolitan fast lines were on the outside with the Bakerloo in the middle. The Bakerloo then took over the operation of the Stanmore branch, including the burrowing junction built north of Wembley Park which eliminated the problems created at this station by the previous expansion.

The Bakerloo service began working to Stanmore on 20 November 1939, stations being provided at Acacia Road (named St. John's Wood), situated between the Metropolitan stations of Marlborough Road and St. John's Wood (which had been renamed Lords only a few months previously) and at Swiss Cottage. Marlborough Road and Lords were closed when the Bakerloo trains began working, but the Metropolitan platforms at Swiss Cottage remained operational until 17 August 1940.

The re-arrangement of the fast tracks on either side of [69]

61 *The locomotive change at Rickmansworth about 1960. The electric locomotive is approaching to couple to a London-bound train. The steam locomotive which has brought the train from Aylesbury is returning to the coaling sidings at the north end of the station. The operation took several minutes*

the slow tracks was extended north of Wembley Park for Metropolitan trains. It was not desirable to rebuild again Preston Road and Northwick Park stations, although a complete rebuilding of Harrow-on-the-Hill station could not be avoided. Unfortunately the Second World War interrupted the work and track re-arrangement was stopped north of Preston Road. A flat crossing of the 'Up' or southbound fast line over the slow lines remained in use until 8 March 1948, a few weeks before the enlargement of Harrow-on-the-Hill station to the six-track layout at present in use.

The 1935/40 Programme had also envisaged the duplication of the tracks north of Harrow to Rickmansworth, as well as the extension of the electrification beyond Rickmansworth at least to Amersham. The planning and acquisition of the necessary land was in fact well ahead when work was stopped in the autumn of 1939 because of the outbreak of war. The project then remained in abeyance until 1956 when the work was recommenced. The scheme was by then modified but included the electrification to Amersham and the withdrawal of Metropolitan trains beyond this point.

At North Harrow, Pinner, and Northwood Hills the additional tracks were built clear of the existing platforms; the arrangement of having the slow trains between the fast trains was not continued beyond Harrow.

At Northwood, room was not available on the west side of the existing station so that a change-over of tracks had to be arranged and the old station demolished. The first stop for the fast trains north of Harrow was arranged at

62 *Interior of Neasden Depot, about 1952 after the rebuilding, showing the multiplicity of stocks*

Moor Park, where a completely new station was built with separate island platforms for the fast and local tracks. The Watford branch junction, opened on 2 November

the Chesham branch ran on the night of 11/12 September 1960. Electric locomotives continued to haul through Aylesbury steam trains with the locomotive change at Rickmansworth until 9 September 1961, when Amersham became the northern terminus of all Metropolitan Line

63 *Four-tracking Wembley Park to Harrow—diagram*

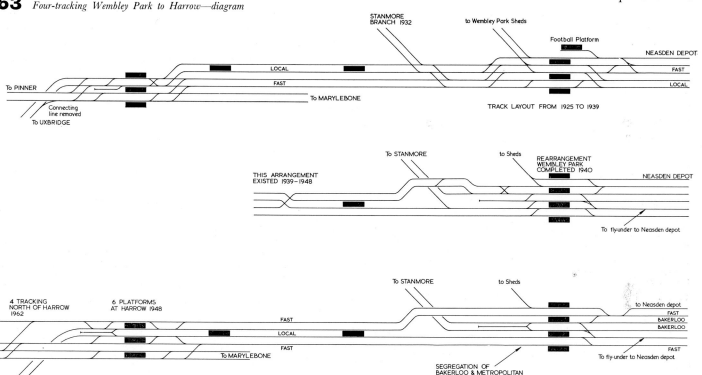

1925, was only provided on the local tracks, beyond which the local and fast tracks converged for entry into Rickmansworth.

The first electric train reached Amersham on 15 August 1960 and the last Metropolitan steam passenger train on

trains. The four-tracking work including the new station at Moor Park was not, however, completed until 17 June 1962.

18 | Main Line Electrification— additional Stock

Through trains were worked from Baker Street to Harrow and Uxbridge, by electric traction from 1 January 1905, and, with the improved service provided, traffic at intermediate stations began to increase. Consideration eventually had to be given to providing an increase in the available rolling stock so that the train service could be augmented.

The electrification of the lines south of Harrow, however, had rendered most of the steam stock surplus to requirements. At that time, this consisted of four different train compositions: (a) rigid wheelbase 8-wheeled stock, (b) twin carriage stock, (c) 'Jubilee' stock, and (d) 'Bogie' stock. With the exception of the 'Bogie' stock most of the other stock was stored. Even all the 'Bogie' stock was not required to maintain the steam stock service, and arrangements were made to provide two train sets for electric services from this group of stock

to be powered by using 150 BWE saloon motor cars.

These sets, which went into service early in 1906, were generally made up with the motor car at the 'down' end of the train coupled to four 'Bogie' stock coaches. This arrangement was proposed so that the motor car could be uncoupled at Harrow and the rake sent on behind a steam locomotive outside the electrified territory. To enable this train formation to work in both directions the brake van in the set was converted to a driving trailer. Full driver's look-out windows of an unusually large size were provided and the cars were fitted with BWE 9-core control line and the Westinghouse brake equipment. At the end, coupled to the motor car, a centre buffer was provided but the screw coupling arrangement was retained for attachment to the steam locomotive.

It was found in practice that the 150 BWE motor cars were not sufficiently powerful for this duty, and the sets were modified to take 200 BTH motor cars.

With the advent of the 'Dreadnought' steam stock more 'Bogie' stock became available and it was decided to convert two complete train sets of seven coaches for electric working. Four brake coaches were each equipped

64 *'Bogie'-stock train as converted to electric working outside the old car shed at Neasden. Double stepboards are still fitted to the trailer coaches*

with four GE69 traction motors, type 200 BTH equipment and new motor bogies of the Fox pressed steel type, with 7 ft. wheelbase and 38-inch diameter wheels. The coaches of the trains were equipped with traction voltage lighting (five lamps in series) and heating, but through control of this installation was not provided, local switches being fitted at the ends of the vehicles. The BTH 10-core control line was fitted on both the 'Up' and 'Down' side so that the coaches were interchangeable and reversible. The trains were fitted with the Westinghouse air brake.

The passenger compartments on the motor coaches were reduced at first from five to four, to allow the original luggage space to house the control equipment and for one passenger compartment to become a luggage compartment. To afford adequate ventilation for the resistance banks, torpedo-type ventilators were fitted to the roof over the new switch compartment as well as side louvres. Subsequently the passenger compartments were reduced to three, the fourth one being used exclusively by the guard.

The first train of this type in 7-car formation went into service on the Uxbridge line on 11 July 1906. It was originally intended that seven trains should be converted, but only two were completed. The trains were subsequently increased to eight coaches when the platform lengthening programme in the inner area was completed. Some of the platforms were still very short for trains of this length (about 330 feet), and it was at this time that arrangements were made to use another passenger compartment in the motor cars for the guard in order to bring him nearer the centre of the train. A door into the luggage compartment was provided from this compartment.

The trains, when composed of seven cars, seated 400 passengers—280 Third Class and 120 First Class. With the addition of one Third Class trailer but the loss of two compartments converted to guard's compartments, the accommodation was increased by 50 passenger seats. The compartments accommodated only five aside in a body width of 8 ft. 3 in. The trailer cars were coupled by short links but the motor coaches were coupled to them by screw couplings. These trains were subsequently designated 'M' stock in the Metropolitan timetables. [73]

65 *The same train after the formation of London Transport*

66 *'William Ewart Gladstone', No. 10, with original nameplate*

67 *The same locomotive with the 'Aylesbury' Pullman*

Second Class accommodation was withdrawn with electric services in 1905, and by 17 December 1906 all the steam service had been converted.

In 1907 an agreement was reached with the District which required the transfer of saloon motor cars, especially the 200 BTH type, to the Circle service. This depleted the 'semi-converted' sets of their motive power, and it was then decided to add four more 'Bogie' stock coaches to the rakes and fully convert them to electric working, making two 6-car trains. These trains were designated 'N' stock in the Metropolitan timetable classification.

The vehicles converted to motor coaches were the two driving trailers and two vehicles which had been stored after being used in the Wembley Park electrification experiment. They were fitted with the 150 BWE equipments which had been taken into storage after orders had been placed for BTH equipments. All the trailer coaches were fitted with BTH 10-core control lines so that they could be generally interchangeable with the other trains of this type.

The BWE motor cars with their 9-core control were coupled by means of special jumper connections. The two 6-car sets were made up as follows:

3M–3T–3T–1T–3T–3M

providing a seating capacity of 330 with 270 Third Class and 60 First Class. These sets were worked on the Uxbridge service until 1932 when, with the opening of the Stanmore branch, they were reduced to 4-car formations for this service until it was taken over by Bakerloo tube stock.

Arising from the train formation then operating on the Circle, some trailer saloon cars were rendered redundant and, with the delivery of the new electric locomotives, three trains of five vehicles were made up for operating local trains to Neasden. Having end doors only and fewer seats than the other trains then operating, these trains were unpopular and caused public complaint. In 1909 three sets of 'Jubilee' stock were taken out of storage, each set consisting of nine coaches providing 390 seats, 80 First Class and 310 Third Class. These were fitted with traction type lighting and heating. Shoebeams were fitted to the brake coaches to provide the supply to lighting and heating but the bus line provided was not suitable for traction current and was not connected to the locomotive, so that gapping of these trains was not infrequent. These trains were successful in meeting the traffic needs so that it was decided to provide a further three trains. These were composed of six vehicles of old straight-sided 8-wheeled non-bogie stock which had been stored, and were given similar treatment being provided with traction lighting and heating. The trains of this make-up hauled by electric locomotives ran in service until 1912/13, when it was possible to re-arrange the service with more modern rolling stock.

19 The Electric Locomotives of the Metropolitan

Unlike the District Railway, which arranged for the complete electrification of its system, the Metropolitan envisaged dual working arising from the services extending well into the country area. The Metropolitan decided, therefore, to build some electric locomotives capable of hauling the heaviest steam passenger trains over the electrified tracks, as it was considered desirable to eliminate all steam working into Baker Street.

The first 10 locomotives were ordered from the British Westinghouse Electric & Manufacturing Company and built by the Metropolitan Amalgamated Railway Carriage Company at Saltley under sub-contract. All these locomotives were delivered and ready for service by April 1906. They were double bogie vehicles with a central cab having bonnets at either end, a type of locomotive normally described as 'camel backed'. The length over buffers was 35 ft. 9 in. with bogie centres at 17 ft. 3 in. The bogies of pressed steel had a wheelbase of 7 ft. 6 in. and each carried two type 86M nose-suspended traction motors, driving 36-inch diameter wheels through spur gearing with a ratio 22/60. These motors were of the Westinghouse split-frame design, without interpoles but with plain split sleeve bearings. The advantage of this type of motor was that the armature, which required a great deal of maintenance in these early years, could be removed without lifting the vehicle. These motors were expected to work under very arduous conditions and cooling was increased by providing a motor-driven blower for forced ventilation.

Each pair of motors was controlled by 15 electro-pneumatic switches in the form of a turret actuated by a low voltage supply, powered by a 14-volt battery. A single small master controller was originally installed to control both sets of equipment, but was not arranged for automatic acceleration because of the amount of shunting the locomotives were expected to do. The provision of only one control position was found to be unsatisfactory for locomotives requiring to travel in both directions with equal facility without recourse to a turntable, since the driver was badly placed for good visibility in one direction of travel. An additional master controller was fitted soon after delivery of the vehicles.

The locomotives were fitted with an electrically-driven air compressor and two exhausters. The compressor provided compressed air for the Westinghouse brake equipment and the pneumatically-operated control gear. The locomotives were designed to haul trains fitted with either the Westinghouse or the vacuum brake and were themselves dual fitted. The Gresham & Craven or Reavell exhausters were provided in tandem working at full and half speeds. When coupled to a vacuum-braked train, the exhauster on half-speed worked continuously to maintain the vacuum against normal train line leakages while the full-speed machine was switched in when a brake release was required. On the locomotive only one brake block on each wheel was provided, but this was actuated by either system of brake operation.

The bogies were each originally fitted with transverse beams at the outer ends but located on the axle boxes to carry the collector shoes, positive on the outside with a negative in the middle. This type of gear gave trouble on the car stock on the Circle, so all vehicles were subsequently modified to the conventional arrangement with the positive shoebeam mounted between the axle boxes and the negative from the motor casing at its outer end.

One very distinctive feature of these locomotives was the large roller destination blind displaying 12-inch lettering carried at both ends, extending the whole width of the body. The blinds must have given trouble because they were removed at an early stage in the life of the locomotives. Automatic couplers were not fitted, coupling to trains being by link and screw, the standard main line practice.

The 'turret' type control system on both the car stock and these locomotives was not satisfactory and was replaced by individual electro-pneumatic contactors. The 14-volt battery was also replaced by a motor generator set. This work was not completed on all locomotives until 1911.

Following the experience with the first 10 locomotives a contract was placed in 1906 for a further 10 vehicles from the same car builders, but this time BTH electro-magnetic traction control equipment was specified. In addition a box-like body with the driver's controls at the outer ends was arranged. These vehicles were lighter at 47 tons and shorter, being only 33 ft. 6 in. over buffers

against 50 tons of the BWE locomotives, which were over 2 feet longer.

Two sets of type 200 BTH (GE69) equipments were provided; the master controllers were fitted with dead-man's handle, although it was always the practice to carry two men in the electric locomotives and this feature was rarely used in service. Although multiple operation of two locomotives of the same type would have been feasible, through control lines were not provided on either type. The BTH locomotives were provided with buck-eye couplers as well as the standard screw coupling. The latter was removable, being carried in the cab when not required. The first BTH type locomotive entered service in September 1907.

Experimental haulage of steam trains by electric locomotive began in 1906, and by 1 November of that year all trains were hauled electrically from Baker Street as far as Wembley Park where engine changing was arranged. Harrow-on-the-Hill station was reconstructed to four platforms on 21 June 1908, and from 19 July of the same year the locomotive exchange was transferred to this [77]

68 *The 'Down' Pullman racing the 'Down' Manchester express near Northwick Park*

point. This remained the end of the electrified territory until 5 January 1925 when the locomotive exchange point was transferred to Rickmansworth on the extension of the electrification. This remained the transfer point for locomotive-hauled stock until electric locomotives were withdrawn from passenger service.

The equipment of the BTH locomotives proved very satisfactory, requiring no modifications at all, but in 1913 this equipment was removed and fitted to new car stock then being constructed, and 10 sets of BWE equipment ordered for these cars were fitted to these locomotives. This was done, it was said, to maintain a rolling stock balance between BWE- and BTH-equipped trains.

The replacement work included the transfer of trucks and traction motors. The new bogies had 86M type split-frame traction motors fitted with a wheelbase of 7 ft. 9 in. All 20 locomotives now had similar equipments but different appearance.

In 1919 it was decided that it was necessary to improve the power available for hauling steam trains as these were becoming heavier by the provision of longer trains with improved amenities. As part of the plan of re-equipment of the Metropolitan Railway it was decided to rebuild the 20 electric locomotives giving them an improved performance. After the completion of a trial locomotive (No. 17) the rebuilding plan was abandoned as being unsatisfactory, and new locomotives were purchased from Vickers Ltd. of Barrow. Metropolitan-Vickers, the successor to the British Westinghouse, was the main contractor supplying the new electro-magnetic control gear and the MV339 type traction motors, each with a nominal rating of 300 h.p. The 86M motors supplied in 1913 had been rated at 215 h.p. on the comparative one-hour basis. The MV339 motors were, in fact, the largest ever to be used on London Transport service. As

originally built they were provided with sleeve bearings but had interpoles and solid frames. In 1953, because of the postponement of the electrification plans beyond Rickmansworth, a sufficient number of these motors was modified and fitted with roller bearings when a renovation of 15 remaining locomotives was undertaken at Acton Works. The fitting of roller bearings was a necessary step in the reduction of maintenance procedures as grease-lubricated roller bearings could run up to 12 months without regreasing, although oil-lubricated sleeve bearings required attention every few days and renewal under 12 months. Because of the size of the traction motors, the new bogies were arranged with larger diameter wheels—$43\frac{1}{2}$ inches when full size. The gear ratio provided was 23/57. The locomotives were much heavier than the earlier types; their total weight in working order was $61\frac{1}{2}$ tons. Screw couplings were normally provided, but buck-eye couplings could be fitted and were carried inside the locomotives.

Locomotive No. 15 was placed on view at the Wembley Empire Exhibition in 1924 and was given a nameplate recording the fact. In 1926 it was decided to name all the locomotives and cast-bronze plates were installed with the various names bestowed on the locomotives. In 1943, as a result of a suggestion to help the war effort, it was decided to remove these bronze plates for scrap, but there was considerable reluctance to do this immediately because extensive renovation work was necessary after removal of the plates. The work could only be adequately carried out when the vehicles passed through Acton Works for overhaul, with the result that the last plate was not removed until 1948!

In 1953, 15 working locomotives were left in the fleet and a complete renovation was undertaken at Acton Works. Nameplates were again fitted! In addition to the fitting of roller bearings to the traction motors mentioned above, the Metro-Vick traction control equipment was replaced by BTH electro-magnetic type available from the scrapping of District Line cars. More modern compressors were also fitted. These loco-motives were fitted with exhausters, a vacuum brake control line, brake valve and vacuum brake cylinders, but this brake was used only for controlling the train. The Westinghouse brake was normally used on the locomotive itself. As originally installed, both the Westinghouse and vacuum brake cylinders had actuated leverages which applied the brakes on both trucks together. Following the renovation work at Acton it was considered desirable to alter this arrangement because of the necessity for these vehicles to work as single units. To avoid the possibility of a dangerous brake failure when operating as a single vehicle the main brake beam was divided, each part being separately actuated so that each truck was virtually independently braked. Only one locomotive was not given back its original name; Locomotive No. 2, which had been *Oliver Cromwell* was renamed *Thomas Lord*. The recent war against dictators had left its mark! The full name William Ewart Gladstone was curtailed on the appropriate new nameplate to *W. E. Gladstone*.

The locomotives were principally used for hauling the Aylesbury, Verney Junction, and Chesham trains within the electric territory, but saw many other duties as well. They hauled the through passenger trains composed of Great Western coaches from Paddington to the City until 16 September 1939, when due to war conditions this service ceased. At one time three such trains were worked in the morning and evening peaks. There were some goods train workings to Vine Street Goods Depot and the coal train to feed the boiler house at Chiltern Court.

Although the electrification to Amersham was com-

69 *The driver's controls of a 1920-type locomotive. The vacuum brake handle is to the left of the Westinghouse brake handle*

pleted on 12 September 1960, through trains to Aylesbury continued for another year. Locomotives were still changed at Rickmansworth to avoid providing facilities for the locomotives at Amersham. However, through Chesham trains were electric locomotive-hauled all the way during this time until replaced by multiple unit stock.

Four locomotives were retained for shunting duties, one at Acton Works, Neasden, Ealing Common, and Ruislip. After the final delivery of the 'A' stock the locomotive at Ruislip was scrapped; the remaining three still perform intermittent duty as required. Locomotive No. 1 *John Lyon* was brought up to exhibition condition for the Metropolitan Railway Centenary at Neasden in 1963, and No. 5 *John Hampden* hauled the commemorative special.

[79]

20 | The Rothschild Saloons and the Pullmans

The extension of the Metropolitan line from Chalfont Road to Aylesbury was opened on 1 September 1892. Wendover, one of the stations on this line, was near the country seat of the millionaire Ferdinand de Rothschild. He began to patronize the new railway facilities, reserving a First Class compartment for his requirements. In 1895, however, the Metropolitan Railway ordered from Brown Marshalls two special saloon vehicles which could be formed into a special train to accommodate this First Class passenger and his entourage.

These vehicles were 32 feet long and were provided with six wheels equally spaced; the only Metropolitan vehicles ever to be built with this arrangement which was considered to provide a very smooth ride. One of the Royal Trains of this period was also provided with six-wheeled coaches for the same reason. At one end of one saloon there was a six-foot wide compartment and lavatory. There was a luggage section at the other end. The saloons themselves were provided with settees and two armchairs, together with gas lighting. A special train containing these two vehicles was regularly operated for a number of years, but following electrification at the Baker Street end of the line with increased track occupation, it was suggested that this special train should work into

70 *The Rothschild saloon in the train shed at Neasden*

Marylebone. In 1905 these two vehicles went into Neasden Works for extensive overhaul and reconstruction. The old bodies were spliced together to make one vehicle some 58 feet long over the buffers containing two saloons. The virtually new vehicle was provided with four-wheel bogies and Stone's electric lighting system. The saloons were refurnished with movable chairs and tables in place of the fixed settees. This vehicle was known for many years as the 'Rothschild Saloon', and in its later years was used by the Chairman and Directors of the Metropolitan Railway for line inspections. The last official use of the vehicle was to convey the Chairman and officers of the London Passenger Transport Board on an inspection of the Brill Branch before its closure. This saloon was withdrawn from the active stock list in 1935, but remained available at Neasden for over 10 years before it was scrapped. There was a genuine reluctance to break it up.

The Metropolitan Railway felt that the competition from the better-equipped Great Central Railway trains running over the same tracks might cause a depletion of the First Class traffic from the outer areas. As a special inducement to this traffic a 10-year agreement was drawn up, in 1909, with the Pullman Car Company for the introduction of a Buffet Car service.

Two vehicles were built by the Birmingham Railway Carriage & Wagon Company for the Pullman Car Company, but were fitted out to the requirements of the Metropolitan Railway. The cars were just over 59½ feet long over the buffers and had bogies with 7 ft. 6 in. wheelbase. The wheels when new were 40⅝ inches in diameter for maximum riding comfort commensurate with the curvature of the track.

Accommodation was provided in each car for 19 passengers in upholstered armchairs, the saloon itself being divided in three sections containing 8, 7, and 4 seats. In addition to the provision of a small pantry a lavatory was also provided. The lavatory was locked and not available for use in the tunnels south of Finchley Road.

When equipped with seating and furnishings the vehicles weighed 29 tons, and were finished in the Pullman livery of the time—umber bodywork, with upper panels of light cream and gold lining. The interior decoration of the two cars, while similar in treatment, was distinctive but of 18th-century style. One of these handsome cars had a mahogany finish with inlaid satinwood and green upholstery. The other had an oak finish and crimson upholstery. Eight glass-topped tables with portable electric table lamps, typical of the standard Pullman design, were also provided. The outside appearance of the cars contained six square side lights with an oval window at each end. Access to the cars was obtained from the end vestibules.

The cars were coupled in the trains by means of the centre screw link and standard side buffer arrangement. The cars themselves were provided with end doors but these were never used on the Metropolitan, access to the cars being obtained from the station platforms.

The names which were chosen for the two cars, *Mayflower* and *Galatea,* do not seem to have had any special significance to the Metropolitan Railway, and the reason for the choice of names is obscure. These were the two contestant yachts in the 1886 America's Cup.

The Pullman service began on 1 June 1910, and was the first electrically-hauled Pullman service in Europe. Initially the vehicles were formed in trains of 'Bogie' stock necessitating the coupling vehicle being provided with long buffers and screw couplings. Subsequently the vehicles were reformed in trains made up with 'Dreadnought' vehicles, and they remained in these formations until [81]

71 ABOVE—*Pullman car 'Galatea' in original livery at the carbuilder's works*

72 BELOW—*The 'Mayflower' in later livery*

finally withdrawn on 7 October 1939. They were equipped with through electrical bus lines so that the trains containing these vehicles operated under normal conditions when hauled by electric locomotives in the electrified territory. The braking system was, of course, vacuum, to conform with the standard steam rolling stock.

The supplementary fare charged for the use of the Pullman facilities was 1/- beyond Rickmansworth and 6d. for any distance between Aldgate and Rickmansworth. The trains worked from Verney Junction, Aylesbury, and Chesham to Baker Street, certain workings being extended to Liverpool Street or Aldgate. Light refreshment was served, including breakfast, on the inward morning trains. A light supper was served on the late train from Baker Street to cater for the theatre traffic. The supplementary fare was reduced in 1915 for a time to 6d. all the way. When the Pullman cars were withdrawn for overhaul, the Rothschild saloon was used as a substitute to maintain the continuity of the service.

Following the 1922/23 overhaul of the vehicles the external colour scheme was changed to a crimson lake all over, as the light cream was difficult to maintain under the tunnel conditions of the Metropolitan, and this livery was retained until the coaches were withdrawn. They received only one overhaul, at Acton Works in 1935, after the formation of the London Passenger Transport Board.   [83]

73 *Interior of Pullman. The ornate fittings were regilded during the overhaul of the car*

21 | The 1913 Metropolitan Stock and consequent changes

Following the rebuilding of Baker Street station enabling the through running trains to the City, and the electrification of the East London Railway, the Metropolitan required some additional rolling stock. An order was placed with the Metropolitan Carriage Wagon & Finance Company for 23 motor cars and 20 trailer cars. The motor cars were all Third Class but the trailers were equally divided between Thirds and Firsts and, in accordance with then existing practice, the First Class cars were driving trailers.

The distinctive feature of these cars, which were 52 ft. 10 in. long overall, was the elliptical roof with raised ventilators. The motor cars seated 38 passengers

[84]

74 *A southbound Metropolitan car stock train crossing the Stanmore branch flyunder at Wembley Park about 1939*

and had a small luggage compartment directly behind the driving cab. The saloon was designed with one pair of hand-operated sliding doors in the centre of the car, together with one end sliding door at the opposite end to the driver's cab on each side. All the trailer cars, both Thirds and Firsts, seated 48 and were also provided with the middle and end doors. The Third Class had, of course, additional doors where the driving cab door was arranged on the First Class cars.

To equip these cars 23 sets were purchased of duplex 200 BWE type traction equipments for controlling four traction motors, but only thirteen of these equipments were fitted to these new motor cars at Neasden Works. The remaining equipments were fitted to the ten BTH type electric locomotives releasing the 200 BTH (GE69) type equipments for the remaining ten new motor cars.

This division of equipments provided new rolling stock in both types of saloon trains operated by the Metropolitan. These new vehicles were not segregated from the earlier clerestory-roofed stock, and mixed trains of earlier and later built cars were made up in both 200 BTH and 200 BWE type rakes.

The BTH-equipped cars received the bogies from the electric locomotives so that there was some difference in the running gear of the two types of car.

The gear ratio of the BTH cars with GE69 traction motors and 38-inch motor wheels was 19/64, while the BWE cars had 86M traction motors, 36-inch motor wheels and a gear ratio of 22/60. The Fox type pressed-steel trucks from the electric locomotives had a wheelbase of 7 ft. 6 in. while the plate frame trucks taking the 86M traction motor had a wheelbase of 7 ft. 9 in. The trailer trucks provided were similar to those fitted to earlier vehicles which were pressed steel with a 7 ft. wheelbase.

Most of these new cars entered service on the Inner

75 ABOVE—*First Class trailer car of 1912/13 stock. This car later became car No. 9410*

76 BELOW—*A mixed 7-car train of saloon stock, with 1926 Motor Cars*

Circle which now included additional workings to provide the East London service, with four through trains per hour from South Kensington over the Metropolitan side of the Circle. The East London service was actually 12 trains an hour of which eight were shuttle operations from Shoreditch. The car stock on the main line at this time consisted of a number of trains made up into 6- and 7-car formations, whereas on the Circle working the maximum length of a train was usually of four cars.

The traffic on the Metropolitan Railway increased considerably during the war years, and at the end of hostilities there was insufficient rolling stock to meet the needs of all the services—for a time some Great Western vehicles were borrowed and used on the Uxbridge service until additional rolling stock could be obtained. Some time later the luggage compartment was converted for passenger accommodation on 16 of the twenty-three 1913 motor cars. The seating capacity of the cars was raised from 38 to 46 by this means, as well as providing additional standing room. The luggage compartment doorway was sealed up. Normal side lights were not fitted at this time, which made this area somewhat cell-like in appearance, and it was not until the reconditioning work undertaken by London Transport for the improvement of the Circle Line trains that this section of these cars was completely rebuilt.

Most of this stock became part of the fleet used for the Circle working, together with the later 1921 stock, and continued in service until 1952. In order that reference can be made subsequently to the history of some of these cars the following table of the motor cars will be of assistance.

Type of Equipment	Metropolitan No.	London Transport No.
200 BTH (GE69)	83–92	2587–2596
200 BWE (86M)	93–98	2581–2586
	99–105	2546–2552

The reason for the split in the renumbering from the Metropolitan to London Transport arose because the cars working on the Main Line were separately numbered from those working the Circle services. The cars numbered from 2581 to 2596 were retained on the Circle service, but 2589 was severely damaged in a bomb incident in 1941 and the body was replaced by one from an earlier batch of cars, although the number 2589 was retained. Car number 2552 of the batch of cars operating on the main line was transferred to the Circle working after the Charing Cross collision of 17 May 1938, when car number 2546 (a 1921 stock car) was damaged beyond economical repair.

The cars retained for Circle working received a number of modifications before being finally withdrawn in 1952. The cars working on the main line were withdrawn in 1938/39.

22 | The Metropolitan shuttles

In a dense fog at West Hampstead, on 26 October 1907, a serious accident occurred when one 6-car train ran into the back of another. The force of the collision was considerable, there was extensive damage to the colliding vehicles, and three passengers lost their lives in the wreckage. The leading motor car of the colliding train, No. 46, received very severe damage and was stored pending a decision to scrap. No. 46 was a 150 BWE type vehicle.

There was another incident on 6 October 1908 when a severe fire broke out in No. 69, badly damaging its bodywork, and this car was also stored pending a decision to scrap. This car was a 200 BTH type motor car.

In June 1909 No. 46 was used as a gauging car to check clearances for the introduction of the new Pullman coaches which were designed to be rather longer than coaches then in service. A temporary wooden bolster was fitted at one end of the under-frame to enable the bogie centres to be increased to 39 ft. 9 in. from 35 feet. A temporary buffer beam was also fitted to give an equivalent car length of 60 feet.

In 1910 these two cars were converted into double-ended shuttle cars by the Metropolitan Carriage, Wagon & Finance Company, for use on the Uxbridge line from Harrow.

The bodies, 52 feet long, had elliptical roofs with torpedo ventilators and two driving cabs. There were, between the two driving cabs, six compartments and a luggage section with two doors. Two Third Class compartments were placed on either side of the two First Class compartments. The two adjacent Third Class compartments were connected by a central gangway and were not divided by a partition; the middle seating had a luggage rack common to both sides. The passenger accommodation provided for 36 Third Class and 16 First Class—only 50% of each class were smoking. Both cars had a similar appearance but had different electrical equipment.

Car No. 46, which became 2768 in London Transport's numbering scheme in 1933, had 150 BWE equipment with which it had originally been provided. This car retained its 50M type traction motors until scrapped.

Car No. 69, which became 2769, was originally equipped with 200 BTH type equipment. This equipment, being more powerful, would have been wasted on a single shuttle car, so it was interchanged with that of a 150 BTH car, the GE69 traction motors being interchanged for GE76 type. Both these cars were provided with electrical couplings so that they could be attached

[87]

77 *Shuttle car No. 46, afterwards No. 2768. The traction equipment was placed under the solebar, thus no switch compartment was necessary*

to a driving trailer, enabling a 2-car train to be formed when necessary.

These cars were used on the Uxbridge shuttle service until 1918 when they were transferred to the Addison Road shuttle from 12 May of that year. This worked from Edgware Road and had previously been worked by 3-car sets of H. & C. stock. The cars had to be modified at this time because the driver's cab door, as built, had opened outwards like the compartment doors; this was not considered good practice in tunnel operations and these cab doors were altered so that they opened inwards.

After the opening of the Watford branch and the electrification to Rickmansworth these vehicles operated a shuttle between Watford and Rickmansworth round the north curve. This service operated from 2 November 1925 to 21 January 1934, when the vehicles were transferred to operate the off-peak shuttle to Stanmore from Wembley Park. A service by these single units was provided from 21 January 1934 until 27 November 1938, but thereafter, as traffic seemed to have increased, a driving trailer was added permanently to 2769. This worked thereafter as a 2-car set until the service was finally withdrawn on 20 November 1939 on the introduction of the Bakerloo service to Stanmore.

2768 having the less reliable equipment was withdrawn for scrapping in February 1938, but 2769, although not used again in passenger service after November 1939, was retained in reserve until 1942.

[88]

78 *The Ealing Line flyover, looking towards Turnham Green, about 1912*

23 | 1910/13 District Stock—'C', 'D', & 'E' Class

Between 1908 and 1910 a number of important engineering works was undertaken by the District Railway, thus enabling an increased service to be operated which, in turn, required the provision of additional rolling stock.

With the introduction of electric traction a new rolling stock depot was opened at Ealing Common and the workings to and from this yard, together with the operation of the South Acton branch, made the track layout at Mill Hill Park (opened for steam operations in 1879) totally inadequate. A new three-track layout with a

flyover arrangement west of the station (enabling the Ealing service to avoid conflicting with the Hounslow trains, many of which worked from South Acton) was brought into use on 20 February 1910. The station was renamed Acton Town on 1 March of the same year.

Until 3 December 1911 the District Railway had used its running powers over tracks belonging to the London & South Western Railway between Studland Road Junction, just west of Hammersmith, and Turnham Green Junction. This double-track stretch of railway was used by both the London & South Western Railway trains from Richmond to Kensington, and by Great Western trains to Richmond as well as by the District. After electrification of the District the sharing of these tracks with steam trains was very unsatisfactory. The District then arranged for the construction of additional tracks alongside the original London & South Western Railway tracks for its exclusive use. As these would be on the south side of the existing lines, a flying junction

79 *A trailer car, built by Metro-Cammell in 1912*

[89]

80 *A motor car built by Gloucester in 1914, on the traverser at Acton Works some years later*

for the Ealing trains to cross the LSWR tracks at Turnham Green was also included in the proposals.

A new station at Stamford Brook was opened on 1 February 1912, but served by the District trains only. The new track arrangement enabled an improved District Line train service to be operated from 11 December 1911. Subsequently it was considered that all the expense of the additional trackage had really been wasted, because the London & South Western Railway reduced its train service and finally withdrew the Kensington service altogether on 3 June 1916. The Great Western service from Notting Hill (now Ladbroke Grove) was withdrawn on 31 December 1910 so that these tracks were then virtually unused. However, this lack of use paved the way for the adoption of these tracks by the Underground, so that the four-tracking arrangement as in use today was established, enabling the Piccadilly Line to be projected west of Hammersmith.

In addition to these works, another burrowing junction was constructed at Earl's Court to enable the Wimbledon services to be segregated from those proceeding to Hammersmith. This junction was brought into operation on 4 January 1914. This was the second burrowing junction at Earl's Court; an earlier one at Cromwell Curve east of the station had been constructed to enable the steam trains from High Street Kensington to avoid conflicting with Mansion House trains. This junction had been operating from 1 February 1878.

In addition to the need to provide more trains arising from these major operating improvements some trains were increased in length from seven to eight cars. The installation of automatic electro-pneumatic signalling in the congested area enabled a considerable reduction in headways to be achieved, and advantage was taken of this to introduce into the timetables the so-called 'Non Stop' trains. This system commenced on 16 December 1907 and was a feature of District Line working in some form until 1964. It was said that when this arrangement was introduced the journey time for some trains from Mansion House to Ealing Broadway was reduced from 48 to 30 minutes. This improvement in timing, however, could only be achieved by some trains, and required careful timetabling and timekeeping. Frequently the 'Non Stop' trains did not stop at the station but had to stop subsequently in the tunnel. The term 'Non Stop' was also a misleading description as the trains stopped at most stations, only passing a few in an accepted pattern. The cars were provided with 'Non Stopping' boards on the sides near the doorways which displayed names of the stations at which the trains did not stop. These boards continued to be a feature of all District rolling stock until the 'R' stock in 1947.

To meet the increase in rolling stock required to gain full advantage of these improvements, cars were obtained from three different carbuilders. This group of cars, although generally similar, had a number of distinctive features. In spite of these, in later years this whole group were known as 'Hurst Nelsons' although only the first batch came from these Scottish carbuilders.

An order was placed in 1910 with Hurst, Nelson & Co. of Motherwell, Scotland, for 32 motor cars and 20 trailers. These cars, designated 'C' stock, were delivered in 1911. Both the motor and trailer cars were similar in appearance and construction, and in 1928 the 20 trailers were converted at Acton Works into motor cars. Although the cars were basically constructed of steel, a great deal of wood was used in the bodywork.

The vehicles were 49 ft. 6 in. long with a pair of narrow doors in the middle and single end doors as well. The interior was provided with a clerestory roof and the cars resembled the 'B' class.

The electrical equipment originally supplied by the BTH was of the non-automatic electro-magnetic type similar to that already established on the 'B' class rolling stock. However, the traction motors fitted were of a new type designated GE212, which had interpoles. These were the first such motors to be supplied to the Underground and probably the first such motors to be used in England.

The motor truck was of pressed steel construction and

designated 'B' type while the trailer truck which had a 7 ft. wheelbase was designated 'L' type.

The second batch of cars, 30 in all consisting of 22 motors and 8 trailers, ordered from the Metropolitan Amalgamated Railway Carriage & Wagon Co., were similar in general design. These cars were built in 1912 and were designated 'D' stock. The motor bogies were again 'B' type but a new trailer truck, the 'M' type, was introduced. The eight trailers were also converted to motor cars at Acton Works in the 1928 Reconstruction Programme.

The third batch, the 'E' class or 1913 'Gloucester' stock, was delivered in 1914, again being a total of 30 cars: 26 motors and 4 trailers which also became motor cars in the 1928 Reconstruction Programme. The appearance of these cars was very different because for [91]

81 *Interior of Gloucester-built car*

the first time an elliptical roof construction was provided instead of a clerestory. When first delivered they had small torpedo-type ventilators in the roof which were later removed because they caused too much draught, or resulting in passenger complaint.

The Gloucester cars were provided with a new type motor bogie, the 'C' type, with a 7 ft. 3 in. wheelbase, while the trailer bogie provided was the 'M' type.

The general arrangements of the 'C', 'D', and 'E' class of rolling stock were similar, and although various different types of bogies were originally provided they were all interchangeable, and some mixing of these inevitably occurred when repairs were undertaken. The original bogies gave a great deal of trouble and between 1910 and 1922 at least 60 new motor bogies were provided.

The last batch of these cars was received in time for the District Railway to provide a service of trains from Earl's Court to Willesden Junction, on behalf of the London & North Western Railway, from 1 May 1914 to 22 November 1914 when the North Western rolling stock was delivered following the electrification of this line. This was the remaining portion of the Outer Circle service which continued in operation until 1940 when the service was withdrawn, although the Olympia shuttle does cover a small part of this route.

At this time all cars were interchangeable in duty and formation with the exception of the original 'A' stock. The 'A' stock was confined to the shuttle services at the west end of the line to South Harrow (to Uxbridge from 1 March 1910), and from South Acton to Hounslow.

In May 1908 a 9-car train formation was operated on the Barking line, consisting of four motor cars and five trailers. The three leading cars proceeded from Whitechapel as a 'Non Stop' train to Mansion House; the remaining six cars continued as a normal train. In 1910 some 12-car trains dividing into two 6-car trains were similarly operated. A 9-car train was still running from East Ham to Whitechapel in 1918.

The success of the longer trains at the eastern end of the District Line caused a number of such operations to be tried from Ealing Broadway. In 1914, a 9-car train was operated, with the extra car in charge of a special attendant with passenger access available only at Ealing Broadway, Acton Town, Turnham Green, Hammersmith, and Mansion House. This train operated from June 1914

[92]

82 *Ealing Common lifting shop; 'C' class car in left foreground with an 'E' stock behind and a new 'R' stock being prepared for service on the adjacent road, probably 1950*

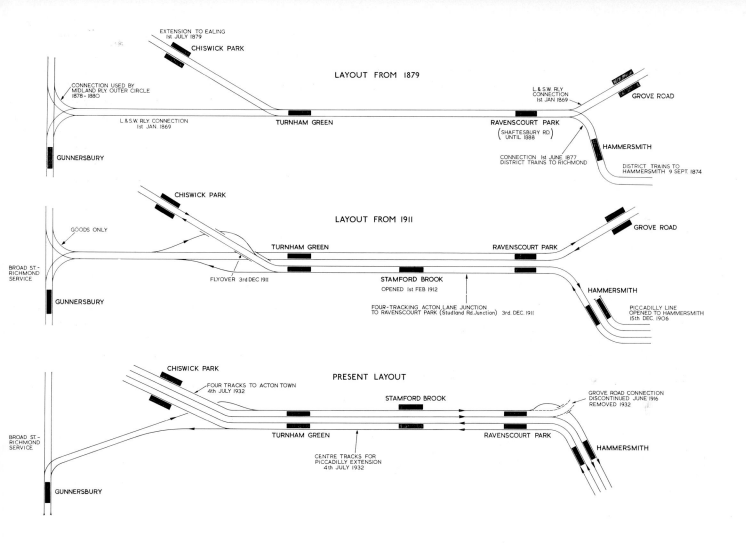

EXTENSION TO EALING
1st JULY 1879

CHISWICK PARK

LAYOUT FROM 1879

CONNECTION USED BY
MIDLAND RLY. OUTER CIRCLE
1878-1880

L. & S.W. RLY
CONNECTION
1st JAN. 1869

GROVE ROAD

L. & S.W. RLY. CONNECTION
1st JAN. 1869

TURNHAM GREEN

RAVENSCOURT PARK
(SHAFTESBURY RD.)
UNTIL 1888

HAMMERSMITH

GUNNERSBURY

CONNECTION 1st JUNE 1877
DISTRICT TRAINS TO RICHMOND

DISTRICT TRAINS TO
HAMMERSMITH 9 SEPT. 1874

CHISWICK PARK

LAYOUT FROM 1911

GOODS ONLY

GROVE ROAD

BROAD ST.-
RICHMOND
SERVICE

TURNHAM GREEN

RAVENSCOURT PARK

GUNNERSBURY

FLYOVER 3rd DEC 1911

STAMFORD BROOK
OPENED 1st FEB 1912

HAMMERSMITH

FOUR-TRACKING ACTON LANE JUNCTION
TO RAVENSCOURT PARK (Studland Rd. Junction) 3rd. DEC. 1911

PICCADILLY LINE
OPENED TO HAMMERSMITH
15th DEC. 1906

CHISWICK PARK

PRESENT LAYOUT

FOUR TRACKS TO ACTON TOWN
4th JULY 1932

STAMFORD BROOK

GROVE ROAD CONNECTION
DISCONTINUED JUNE 1916
REMOVED 1932

BROAD ST.-
RICHMOND
SERVICE

TURNHAM GREEN

RAVENSCOURT PARK

HAMMERSMITH

GUNNERSBURY

CENTRE TRACKS FOR
PICCADILLY EXTENSION
4th JULY 1932

83 *Turnham Green: 4-tracking diagrams*

until after the outbreak of the First World War.

Although at this time most platforms west of Whitechapel were capable of accommodating only 7-car trains, it was decided to operate a number of 8-car formations and to alter the platform length on the important stations. At others, by accurate stopping with half the front car and half the rear car in the tunnels, such trains could be worked without too much difficulty, but some doors had to be locked.

After the end of the First World War numerous platforms west of Mansion House were adjusted to accommodate eight cars. The short platforms east of Mansion House were provided with cat-walks in the tunnels, but these have always been considered unsatisfactory and the work of improvement still continues.

The trains of 6- and 8-car length were usually made up with an equal number of motor and trailer cars. The formation arrangements, however, were complicated by the need to provide both First and Third Class accommodation as well as smoking and non-smoking sections. The motor cars were generally all Third Class, while some trailers provided First Class smoking and non-smoking accommodation. The ninth car on the long Ealing Broadway trains provided both First and Third Class accommodation.

24 | Metropolitan post-war Electric Stock

At the close of the 1914/18 war, the Metropolitan Railway had to increase the rolling stock fleet. The saloon versus the compartment controversy became of paramount importance because the operating experience with the open saloon cars without centre doors had been very unsatisfactory. Several designs were considered including arrangements for the conversion of the existing saloon cars.

Some sample cars were, in fact, converted at Neasden Works to test the effect of different arrangements especially so far as cost was concerned.

Car No. 32 (LT No. 2501) was the first compromise design. It was reconstructed with a single sliding door of about 3 feet in width in the middle of the body. The seating of the vehicle was reduced from 48 to 46. The car concerned was a 150 BWE type motor car and all the seating was Third Class and smoking.

Car No. 14 (2513), another 150 BWE motor car, was also reconstructed to provide a single sliding door behind the luggage compartment in addition to a pair of centre doors. This re-arrangement reduced the seating capacity of the car to 38.

Neither of these two designs was accepted as the answer to the problem, but the cars remained in this modified condition until withdrawn for scrapping just before the Second World War: 2513 in 1936 and 2501 in 1939.

In 1919 a contract was placed with the Metropolitan Carriage Wagon & Finance Co. to rebuild one 6-car train. The cars selected for this experiment were 150 BWE motor cars Nos. 36 and 44, First Class trailer cars 53 (6535) and 55 (6555), two Third Class trailer cars 35 (9516) and 67 (9531). The two motor cars were converted in 1931 to trailer cars and renumbered 197 and 198 before the formations of London Transport, when they received the numbers 9588 and 9589 respectively. The Metropolitan trailer cars were numbered in a separate sequence to motor cars and these numbers should not be confused with the experimental MV153 motor cars built in 1925.

When returned from the Saltley Works (where the conversion was carried out) these cars had a completely changed appearance, including the provision of elliptical roofs instead of clerestories. The main feature on this train, however, was the provision of five swing doors on each side of the trailer cars and four on the motor cars to improve passenger circulation. A similar arrangement is now common practice on British Railways diesel multiple-unit trains. The swing doors, however, on these experimental cars, did not open between seats but in separate vestibules which were provided with draught screens. The seating capacity of the Third Class trailer cars was raised to 58, although the motor cars which still retained a small luggage compartment had only 41 seats and the First Class control trailers 44.

Numerous innovations to the Metropolitan Railway's method of operation were introduced on this experimental train which earned the sobriquet of 'Hustler'. The lighting and heating switches for the first time were placed under the direct control of the guard, by means of through control lines, and not switched on each car individually. The driver was provided with an automatic window wiper, but this equipment was found to be unreliable and was converted subsequently to hand operation.

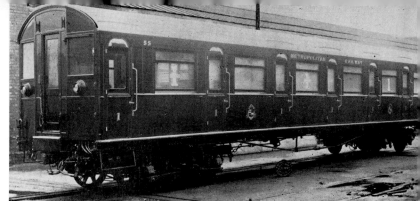

84 *Control trailer car No. 55 after conversion by Metro-Cammell at Saltley in 1919*

Although a considerable amount of publicity was given to this train when it first went into service, a special press inspection being arranged at Baker Street on 18 December 1919, it did not fulfil the expectations and no further cars of this kind were acquired. In 1931, as part of the programme of reducing the number of 150 BWE equipments in service because of the maintenance problems,

[95]

85 *Interior of 'Hustler' trailer car showing partitions at doorways. Compare this interior with the 'C69' stock of fifty years later (Metro-Cammell)*

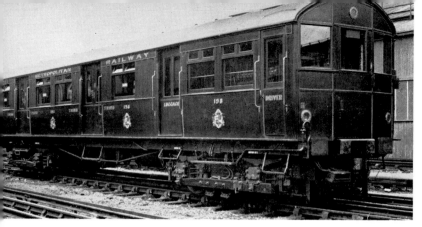

86 *Experimental motor car 198 with the switch compartment behind the driver. The forerunner of the 'MW' stock*

the motor cars of this experimental train were converted to trailer cars. The driving cabs and luggage compartments were removed and the space used to provide additional passenger accommodation. The train was then formed into an 8-car set by providing either two motor cars of 1913 stock or the two 1925 experimental MV motor

[96]

87 *Interior of car 198*

cars as the motive power units. These cars were withdrawn for scrapping in February 1941. This set was known as the 'S' train in the Metropolitan Timetable nomenclature, probably 'S' for special.

In 1921 seven new 6-coach 'Dreadnought' trains were put into service for the steam workings. This enabled a number of 'Bogie' stock vehicles to be withdrawn and converted for electric working. Actually, in 1921, the Metropolitan obtained 101 new vehicles, of which 42 were steam stock. The electric car stock was similar to that purchased in 1913, having elliptical roofs, but the trailer cars of this batch were provided with three pairs of double doors down each side. These doors were hand-operated and gave an opening 4 feet wide.

The motor cars were provided with a small luggage compartment and had a narrower pair of double doors adjacent to this compartment, the other two pairs of double doors being the same size as those provided on trailer cars. There was no through communication from car to car.

The order covered the provision of 20 motor cars, 33 Third Class trailers, and 6 First Class control trailer cars. Most of this stock was used to provide improved service on the Circle workings, a number of the trailer cars being used to increase the length of the trains from four to five cars.

The motor cars were all equipped with 200 BWE equipments and 86M traction motors, which had been recovered from the 20 electric locomotives being replaced by the new Metro-Vick type. The motor cars were, therefore, divided into two classes—one slightly heavier than the other because the pressed steel bogies recovered from the original BWE locomotives were lighter than those fitted to the BTH locomotives, which had plate frame type. There was no difference in appearance but the different bogies had 7 ft. 6 in. and 7 ft. 9 in. wheel-bases respectively, and the unladen weight was 45 tons against 46½ tons.

The motor cars had a seating capacity of 37, the First Class trailer cars 45, while the Third Class trailer cars seated 50. The First Class cars, in addition to having a driving compartment, had a partition dividing the accommodation into smoking and non-smoking. These cars survived in Circle workings until 1947, when with-drawals for scrapping commenced.

A First Class control trailer similar to the 1921 stock was constructed in 1923 for display in the Palace of Engineering at the Wembley Exhibition in 1924/5. This was the last car type trailer vehicle built for the Metro-politan Railway. This vehicle did not become part of the Circle fleet. It was numbered 6557 in London Transport fleet and was used subsequently as part of a 3-car train operating on the East London shuttle service.

25 | The 'MW' Stock, later known as 'T' Stock

Arising out of growth in the Extension traffic following the electrification to Rickmansworth and the opening of the Watford branch on 2 November 1925, additional rolling stock was required.

Fortunately the rolling stock was not immediately necessary as initially the Watford service was shared with the London & North Eastern Railway which provided half the service, steam-hauled, with through trains to Marylebone. The service to Marylebone was subse-quently withdrawn and the Metropolitan then provided the entire service with electrical multiple-unit rolling stock.

At this time the Metropolitan management was still undecided whether to order additional saloon or compart-ment rolling stock for the lengthy journeys now required by the electric stock on the Extension services.

Two experimental motor cars were ordered in 1925 from the 'Metro' company, provided with entirely new equipment designed by Metropolitan-Vickers. The bodies of these cars were substantially the same as the 1921 car stock, but the passenger saloon was shortened by the provision of a switch compartment to accommodate the new type of control equipment. This equipment was electro-pneumatic in operation. The control instructions from the master controller were electrical but the mechani-cal operation of the individual switches was made by means of pneumatic cylinders actuated by the electrically controlled valves. The advantage of this system was basically that the electrical power required for control was small and could be achieved from a low voltage supply, because the mechanical work of operating the switch gear was provided by pneumatic power.

The control supply was provided at 110 volts obtained from a potentiometer across the 600-volt supply. This potentiometer was carried in the roof of the cab behind [97] the driver. The control gear itself was centrally placed in a rack in the special compartment behind the driver, and was duplex. There were two separate sets, therefore, each of which controlled two MV153 traction motors in series-parallel. These traction motors were of 275 h.p. at the one-hour rating which, with a gear ratio of 21/62, made these cars the most powerful multiple-unit vehicles in Europe at the time.

The seating in the vehicles received special consideration and studies were undertaken to obtain the best shape for passenger comfort, a study which under present-day conditions would have been described as ergonomics.

The trucks were of heavy construction, formed of plate and angle, and the axles had journals measuring 11 × 7 inches, the largest so far used on multiple-unit stock. The vehicles weighed just over 49 tons. After the motor cars of the 'Hustler' train were converted to trailer cars these vehicles were generally used to complete the 8-car formation of this set, which was designated 'S'

[98]

88 *'MV'-type motor car 207 (later 2707) with screw couplings, buffers, and vacuum brake pipe. The negative shoe fuse which distinguished these motor coaches from the 'MW' stock is also in evidence*

stock. These two cars were numbered 198 and 199 (2598 and 2599), and later ran on the East London line as a 3-car shuttle train together with the 1924 Exhibition trailer car.

These cars were considered successful and the equipment worked exceedingly well. However, the passengers on the line preferred compartment stock and this fact, together with the length of time taken at terminal stations (especially Baker Street) to unload a crowded train, induced the Metropolitan management to concentrate on compartment stock.

An order was placed for delivery in 1927 with the 'Metro' company for 12 new motor coaches, having five passenger compartments, seating five aside, 50 Third Class passengers in all, a luggage compartment, and a switch compartment as well as accommodation for the driver and guard. These cars were of two types to work with existing trailer stock, because at this time no trailer cars were bought to run with them. The cars were provided with similar Metropolitan-Vickers control equipment, and four MV153 traction motors with a gear ratio of 21/62 giving a balancing speed of 65 m.p.h.

Coach Nos. 200–205 (2700–2705) were provided with Buckeye couplings and no side buffers, which gave an overall length of 53 ft. 9 in. These coaches were fitted with the Westinghouse brake and were used to replace car stock motor cars working with 'Bogie' stock trailers forming the 'W' stock trains. The rakes of 'Bogie' stock had been provided with Buckeye couplings at the outer ends and BTH-type 10-core through control cables, which was satisfactory for the 110-volt system of the new motor coaches. There were three trains made up in this formation.

Coach Nos. 206–211 (2706–2711) were provided with side buffers, screw couplings and vacuum brakes. They had an overall length over couplings of 55 ft. 5 in., although virtually were similar to 200–205. These coaches were used with five coaches of steam stock of the 1920/23 types converted for the purpose to make up three trains of 7-coach length. The conversion consisted of providing a through control line for multiple-unit operation, but in addition six coaches were turned into control trailers by reducing the number of compartments from nine to eight. This enabled the trains to be uncoupled into 3- and 4-coach sets. The three trains made up in this way were designated 'MV' stock. The conversion work undertaken at Neasden was not completed until 1929.

The MV trains of seven coaches were 378 feet long, while those of eight coaches of 'Bogie' stock, the 'W' trains, were 354 feet long. The trailer coaches on the 'MV' trains could still be formed into steam-stock trains if required, while the motor coaches on the 'W' trains could be replaced by open saloon-type motor cars, which gave a limited amount of flexibility when repairs were necessary.

These coaches were considered to be very successful and in 1929 a further batch of coaches were ordered from the Birmingham Railway Carriage & Wagon Co. The total order this time was for 55 vehicles of which 30 were motor coaches with similar Metropolitan-Vickers traction type equipment. The 25 trailer cars were made up with 10 of the motor coaches into five 7-coach trains which became known as 'MW' stock. The 'W' stood for Westinghouse to make a distinction from the 'MV' stock which, although similar in appearance, had vacuum brakes. All the new cars were provided with centre [99]

89 *A 'T' stock train, formerly 'MW' stock*

BAKER ST

90 *A 4-coach 'MW' stock leaving Wembley Park southbound. The original No. 6 platform for Wembley Stadium traffic is on the extreme left, south of the present station*

buffers, and Buckeye couplers so that, in fact, the motor coaches were interchangeable with the first batch of the 1927 stock vehicles.

Coaches No. 212–241 (2712–2741) were, therefore, interchangeable in duties with the original six. Arrangements were made for four of the new motor coaches to be used on 'W' stock trains so that all the trains of this type, of which there were five, were now propelled by the same means, the car stock being released for other duties.

Ten of these latest motor coaches were fitted with roller bearing axle boxes, being the first batch of cars for the predecessors of London Transport with this type of equipment. A number of traction motors too were fitted with roller bearings for the armature, but the motor was axle-hung mounted on the well-tried sleeve type bearings, using the usual waste packing to carry the lubrication to the bearing surface.

In 1931 the last batch of compartment stock for
Underground services was ordered from the Birmingham

Railway Carriage & Wagon Co. This order consisted of 65 vehicles; 18 motor coaches, 14 First Class trailer coaches, 14 control trailer coaches with Third Class accommodation, and 19 plain Third Class trailer coaches. These vehicles were used to make seven complete trains of eight coaches, which had a length of 428 feet, and five of the Third Class coaches were used to increase the existing five 'MW' type train to 8-coach length.

91 *Interior First Class compartment 'MW' stock*

In addition to the fact that these coaches—numbered 242–259 (2742–2759)—were built by a different car builder, the equipment was manufactured by the General Electric Co. However, it was also electro-pneumatic in operation and designed to work in multiple with the Metro-Vick equipment of the earlier cars. The motor bogies were fitted with two motors of type WT545 provided with a gear ratio of 20/62. All axle boxes and traction motors were fitted with roller bearings. Although this arrangement was designed to work in multiple with the MV153 motor having a gear ratio of 21/62, this did not prove satisfactory in practice and these GEC coaches had to be kept segregated.

At the formation of the London Passenger Transport Board there were, therefore, 60 motor coaches, of which a set of six and a set of eighteen were not interchangeable in duties or with each other. So it became necessary to arrange greater interchangeability for better stock utilization. The Metro-Vick gear ratio was changed from 21/62 to 18/65. This arrangement, when applied to the MV153 traction motor, made them compatible with WT545 motors in service which retained the original gear ratio of 20/62.

The three vacuum brake-fitted 'MV' trains were coverted to Westinghouse brakes when they passed through Acton Works during 1935. In addition three steam-stock trailer coaches from the 'Dreadnought' fleet were converted to electric working so that these trains could be lengthened from seven to eight coaches.

There were then 17×8-coach 'MW' stock trains [101]

92 *'MV' stock motor bogie showing the side chains for connecting it to the carbody, and the heavy lay shafts for vacuum brake rigging*

together with 26 motor coaches, which were used as the motive power with other stock in 'W' and 'VT' stock trains. When these trailer cars and coaches were replaced by the introduction of 'P' stock in 1938 seven more steam-stock coaches were converted at Acton Works. The 'MW' stock was then made up into 9 × 8-coach and 10 × 6-coach trains, and this group of stock was then given the designation 'T' stock in London Transport nomenclature. This rolling stock provision, however, only

[102]

93 *Interior of driver's cab of motor car 198*

required 38 motor coaches whereas 60 had originally been built.

At this time it was intended that the additional electric trains required for the extension of the electrification beyond Rickmansworth to Amersham and Chesham would be obtained by converting the 'Steam' stock (the 'Dreadnoughts') to electric working, the motive power being provided by the surplus 'T' stock motor cars. The advent of the Second World War postponed this programme which had also included the fitting of electropneumatic brakes to the 'T' stock. All the motor coaches were kept in running order during the war years so that this work could be completed at the cessation of hostilities.

The provision of through heating and lighting controls was also a feature of the proposed renovation programme. One of the operating disadvantages of the 'T' stock was the fact that heating and lighting switches were operated from the platform by rods at the ends of the vehicles on each coach. One train was actually converted to through controls. The end, however, was in sight, because two of the motor coaches were withdrawn for scrapping before the end of the war. The underframes of these coaches were used for experimental purposes by constructing upon them working 'mock ups' of stock for the future.

The electrification to Amersham was postponed again, and when replacement stock began to be delivered in 1961 the fleet of motor coaches had been gradually reduced to 44. The last 'T' stock train ran in passenger service on Friday, 5 October 1962. Two coaches were retained for the Metropolitan Centenary celebrations before being scrapped. These were 2711 and 9724. Two of the motor coaches, 2758 and 2749, both from the 1932 batch, were converted into a double-unit sleet locomotive for use in winter weather, being renumbered ESL118A and ESL118B respectively.

26 | Renovation of the Circle Stock

At the formation of the London Passenger Transport Board in 1933 the Metropolitan Railway passenger rolling stock transferred to the new organization consisted of:

1. 'Steam' stock, and 20 electric locomotives for working the Aylesbury Line services from the City and Baker Street.

2. Three 7-coach trains of 'MV' stock, compartment-type electric stock with 1927 motor coaches fitted with vacuum brakes.

3. Twelve 8-coach trains of 'MW' stock also compartment type with 1927/30/31 motor coaches but fitted with Westinghouse brakes.

4. Five trains of 'Bogie' stock powered by motor coaches from the 'MW' pool and designated 'W' stock.

5. Five 8-vehicle trains and three 7-vehicle trains also powered by 'MW' type motor coaches, but having saloon trailers marshalled between them. These trains were designated 'VT' stock.

6. One 8-vehicle train made up with the two experimental motor coaches, Nos. 198 and 199, together with the experimental six cars with swing doors like compartments. This train, known as the 'Hustler', had the official designation 'S' stock.

7. Twelve 7-car trains made up with motor cars having either of the 200 BWE or 200 BTH equipments together with saloon trailer cars. The motor cars had, of course, to be used in pairs as they would not 'multiple' with each other. These trains were designated 'V' stock.

8. Two 8-coach trains, provided with motor coaches fitted with 200 BTH equipments, converted from 'Bogie' stock in 1908. These trains were designated 'M' stock.

9. Two 4-coach trains, having the motor coaches fitted with 150 BWE equipments. The trailers of these trains were coupled by short links but the motor coaches were coupled to the rakes by means of screw couplings. These trains were known as 'N' stock.

10. Twenty-three 6-car trains for Hammersmith & City services which included the original H. & C. cars, plus 18 additional cars from the Metropolitan fleet.

11. Eighteen 5-car trains for Circle service, some with BTH and some with BWE equipments.

After the formation of the Board a plan for the renovation of the Circle stock was introduced. During 1934 ninety cars were selected for this duty and were passed through Acton Works for modification. The most striking change was the repainting of the vehicles in a red and cream livery, which altered the appearance of the cars considerably. All the 59 cars of 1921 stock were taken for reconditioning, the remainder being cars of earlier vintage. The selected fleet of 90 vehicles consisted of 36 double-equipped motor cars, 18 control trailer cars and 36 trailer cars. The 18 trains selected were of two basic types, five with 200 BTH motor cars and thirteen with 200 BWE motor cars. The control trailers were not required to be used as such, and the equipment was removed. The 86M type traction motors on the 200 BWE motor cars were not in very satisfactory condition, and it was decided to replace these with secondhand GE212 type motors available from District cars recently scrapped. These motors had solid yokes, interpoles, and had been

[103]

94 ABOVE—*The first 5-car Circle rain with BTH-type 1913 motor cars renovated at Acton Works*

95 BELOW—*Interior of renovated Circle train*

converted to roller bearings. However, because these replacement GE212 motors were rather more powerful than the ones being displaced, it was decided to reduce the actual number of motors on a train from eight to six by converting half of the motor cars to single equipments. These motors had become available from two sources, some from the Watford Joint Stock withdrawn in 1930 and the remainder from District motor cars being converted to trailer cars.

The BTH cars had GE69 motors, which were in better condition because they had solid yokes and were not of the split-frame type which had proved very vulnerable to excessive wear in the bearing housing. The GE69 motors were replaced later by GE212 type when further supplies became available by the introduction of 'Q' stock to the District Line. The gear ratio employed on both types of car was 19/64.

The programme of work included refurnishing of the interior of the cars; loose cushion type upholstery was provided in the First Class and fixed moquette-covered

96 ABOVE—*'BW' type 1921-stock Circle motor car on the turntable at Neasden Depot after repainting in all-red livery*

97 BELOW—*A 5-car Circle train in the Cleaning Shed at Neasden Depot. Car No. 2574, a 'BW' 1921 stock car is still in the two-colour livery*

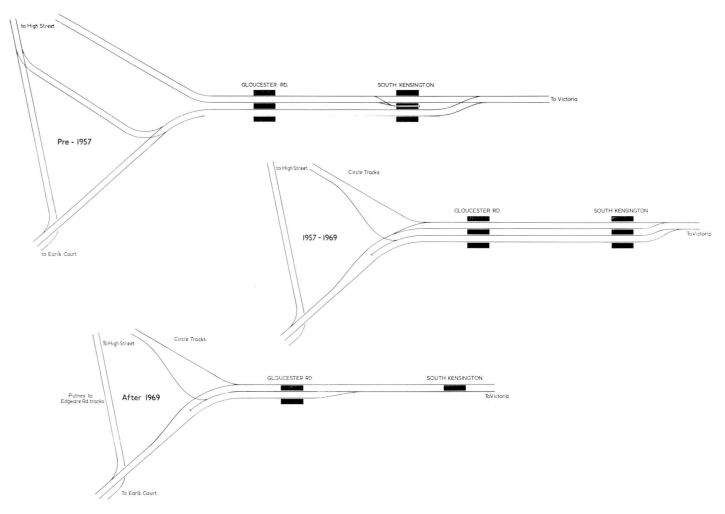

to High Street

GLOUCESTER RD.

SOUTH KENSINGTON

To Victoria

Pre - 1957

to Earl's Court

to High Street

Circle Tracks

GLOUCESTER RD.

SOUTH KENSINGTON

To Victoria

1957 - 1969

To High Street

Circle Tracks

GLOUCESTER RD

SOUTH KENSINGTON

To Victoria

Putney to
Edgware Rd tracks

After 1969

To Earl's Court

98 *South Kensington—Earl's Court diagram*

seats in the Third Class. The control trailers had been retained in the formations because these vehicles provided the First Class accommodation. Lighting fittings were re-arranged and fitted with bell-type shades similar to those used on tube stock at the time. Previously the Metropolitan cars had had unshaded bulbs. The luggage compartments were eliminated, thus increasing the seating accommodation. To bring the vehicles in line with standard practice on the District, communicating doors were installed between the cars so that through detrainment of passengers in an emergency could be arranged.

In addition some of the cars were fitted with K2 bogies in the trailing positions, as this type of bogie had become available from the scrapping of District Line cars. They were much superior to any other trailer bogie then in service. As K2 bogies became available they were not only fitted to Circle stock but also to some 'Steam' stock coaches. These bogies had the advantage of providing double block brake rigging against the single blocking previously employed on these trailer cars.

The traction equipments remained unaltered; the BWE type had electro-pneumatic contactors actuated by a low voltage 24-volt supply obtained from a small motor generator set carried in the driver's cab. The contactor notching under the control of a master controller was provided with automatic acceleration by a notching relay. The BTH cars, on the other hand, had electro-magnetic contactors actuated by 600-volt circuits under the control of a master controller, the driver having to hand-notch through the control sequence without the overriding control of a notching relay.

The cars were originally finished externally in a red and cream livery, and internally in the standard Underground colour scheme of that time of cerulean blue and cream. Subsequently at later overhauls, to reduce the painting costs, the cream upper panels were painted red to provide the overall red colour scheme which the cars retained until scrapped.

The successful repainting of the Circle stock which, without doubt, enhanced the appearance of the cars concerned, caused consideration to be given to repainting all the Metropolitan stock which was to be retained for further service, because the varnished teak finish was an expensive process. Rakes of 'Steam' stock during 1936 received treatment, one set being painted olive green, another Underground red, but both these were uninspiring. The last colour experiment was the painting of a train bright green with a waistband of red. This was particularly horrible and the dark brown finish, resembling as near as possible the original teak, was decided upon as the best compromise which did not alter materially the general appearance of the vehicles.

Five-car 'P' stock trains began to operate on the Circle service in February 1947, and the last Circle Stock train was withdrawn on 31 December 1950.

99 ABOVE—*A 5-car 'F' stock outside Ealing Common Depot*

100 BELOW—*A 2-car 'F' stock compared with 'B' stock outside Acton Works, about 1922. The Paint Shop now stands where the cars are*

27 | 1920 Stock, 'F' Stock —or 'Tanks'

After the end of the First World War, considerable industrial difficulty arose as manufacturers changed over from munition supply to peace-time requirements. The Government of the day provided some assistance in the transition period. One of the benefits to the District Railway from this policy was the provision of 100 new cars. The actual financial arrangement concerning these vehicles is not entirely clear, but they were certainly much more lavish in equipment and appointments than could have been provided by the District Railway finances.

The cars were built by the Metropolitan Carriage, Wagon & Finance Co. at its works in Birmingham and were known officially as 1920 Stock and given the designation letter 'F'. They were known at first as 'Dreadnoughts' but were immediately nicknamed 'Tanks'. Whether this name came from the fact that they were built in shops which had only recently been building parts for such vehicles, or because of their construction almost entirely of steel, will never be resolved. The cars retained this nickname to the end of their days and are still remembered by this name by all who knew them. The first train went into passenger service on 23 December 1920.

These cars were additional to the existing fleet and were always incompatible, being made up into separate trains. From the beginning they were intended to provide additional facilities because some increase in the service

had been made possible by the introduction of colour light automatic signalling. The trains were provided with a high performance as well as a high carrying capacity. The acceleration provided was of the order of 1·5 m.p.h./second which was superior to anything previously operated on the District. It is difficult to appreciate now how this improved performance was to be fully utilized operating among trains which did not have the benefit of these improvements. However, it was considered that they could be utilized to enable the 'non-stopping' services to be improved where the improved performance could be of benefit in short bursts at least.

The original formation was of 8-car length M–T–T–T–M × CT–T–M so that it could be divided into two portions, one of 5-car length and the other of 3-car length, which could operate separately. The motor cars as originally delivered were double equipped, having four traction motors. These were of a new type designated GE260, which were provided with a tapped field system which enabled higher speeds to be achieved. These were the only motors to be operated by the Underground with this system for increasing the motor speed. On all other stock, increases in top motor speed were obtained by a field divert system (generally described as a shunt field system, which is technically incorrect), in which the reduction in field strength of the motor to give the higher running speed was obtained by diverting or shunting a proportion of the current through resistances in parallel with the main motor fields.

The BTH control system was electro-magnetic with individual contactors providing multiple-unit control by means of a hand notching master controller. It is surprising that this advanced rolling stock was provided with a system of control which had already been technically superseded by automatic notching under the control of an accelerating relay. In fact the equipments provided on these trains were obsolete within five years, but in spite of this gave excellent service for 40 years.

The gear ratio of these high-speed motors, which were axle hung, was 19/64. Each pair of motors was controlled in series-parallel by an independent set of equipment, two sets being carried on each car. The trains were intended to be operated at 45 m.p.h. on non-stop runs. In the event they were found to work up to speeds in excess of this and were considered to be overpowered, consuming too much 'juice'. Because of this, arrangements were made for fifteen of the motor cars to be reduced to single equipments which would help to reduce the maximum current at starting. Fourteen of these equipments, together with the traction motors, were then fitted to the seven electric locomotives used on the through Southend trains, improving their performance.

The motor bogie had a long wheelbase of 7 ft. 10 in., while the trailer bogies were of 7 ft. 3 in. wheelbase. These trucks, designated 'E' and 'N' type respectively, were of rolled steel construction, remaining virtually in their original condition for the whole of their life with the exception of the springing. This was considered to be too lively and was replaced subsequently with springs with greater damping.

The actual cars were of all steel construction and were built to templates, so that sections were interchangeable from car to car and very little individual tailoring was incorporated in their construction. The cars were 11 inches wider than previous stocks, the width being increased from 8 ft. 8 in. to 9 ft. 7 in. The body width was extended almost to the limit of the step board of the earlier stock; the sides, however, were slightly inclined above the waist-rail. In addition they were 8 inches longer, being 49 ft. 8 in. overall. The double-equipped motor cars were heavy, weighing 44½ tons. The whole interior of the cars was of steel, but the panels and mouldings were finished to resemble woodwork. As originally delivered the floors were not provided with the usual wood lagging, being covered with linoleum.

The seating capacity of a motor car was 40, a control trailer 44 and a trailer 48. The seats themselves were mainly facing; cross seats were only provided at the end bays. Vertical grab poles were originally provided for the convenience of standing passengers, but in practice these poles were found to be an obstruction and were removed.

Six large ventilators of an improved pattern were fitted in the roof. These were found to be exceedingly draughty and uncomfortable when entering tunnels, and were soon sealed up. During the Second World War the operating handles were found to be useful for attaching the 'reading lights' which were fitted to provide a very slight glimmer of light in the open sections during the hours of darkness as part of the air-raid precaution arrangements. In these cars reading light battens were fixed to the ventilator handles instead of the ceiling. After the reading lights were removed the handles were cut off at ceiling level also. The square-type roof ventilator ducts outside on the roof, however, remained a distinctive feature of the external appearance of these cars. Another special distinctive feature was the oval windows at the car ends, including the driver's look-outs.

Three pairs of double doors, rather narrow and hand-operated, were provided on each car and the trains soon received a well-deserved reputation for clearing large crowds quickly from platforms, and were always in demand for services to cover the football matches at Chelsea and Fulham.

The 100 cars originally ordered were divided into

40 motor cars (12 westbound and 28 eastbound) and 60 trailer cars, of which 12 were control trailers with the control equipment at the westbound end. These control trailers were composite, having both First and Third Class accommodation, as were 12 other ordinary trailer cars, leaving 36 as Third Class cars.

When the fifteen motor cars were reduced to single-equipped vehicles this seems to have been arranged without due regard to the train formations, as the reconstruction programme carried out between 1928 and 1930 included the turning of two double-equipped vehicles and two single-equipped vehicles. The fleet allocation of driving positions then became 12 double-equipped westbound, 15 single-equipped eastbound and 13 double-equipped eastbound motor cars with 12 westbound control trailers. This reconstruction programme, begun in 1928 and completed by June 1930, included the fitting of the electro-pneumatic brake. The first operation in passenger service of this type of equipment in London was June 1928. The train formation at this time was:

$$DM–3T–1T–3T–SM–CT–3T–DM$$

and as the control trailer provided First Class accommodation, this formation gave a symmetrical train in this respect.

The 'F' stock was chosen for the extended trial of the electro-pneumatic brake equipment which had been developed in America, because this block of stock could be kept segregated.

At the time of this reconstruction the lino flooring was replaced with the normal wood lagging, as this was found to be more serviceable.

One train was at first equipped experimentally with the American Westinghouse Type 20 driver's brake valve based on the electro-pneumatic design then in use in

101 *Original interior of 'F' stock, with vertical grab poles*

102 *Interior of 'F' stock in its final form with additional light fittings at the cant rail. The centre grab poles have been removed and the seating provided with armrests* [111]

103 *Driver's cab of 'F' stock with the Type 20 E.P. brake controller on the left*

New York. Between 1928 and 1930 all the 'F' stock was equipped with the Type 21 brake controller which incorporated the full electro-pneumatic control. Subsequently when this equipment was applied to other Underground rolling stock following the success of this trial the American nomenclature was abandoned and the controller used in London Underground became known as the 'A' type. During the third rehabilitation of the 1920 stock in 1950 the Type 21 brake controllers were replaced with type 'A' controllers, many of which had become redundant from the tube stock control trailers no longer required.

In 1938 the second rehabilitation of the 1920 stock was undertaken. The principal work being carried out at this time was the conversion of the control trailers to single-equipped motor cars and the fitting of air-operated doors with passenger push-button control.

The control trailers were converted to motor cars by the transfer of equipment from the scrapped 'Southend' locomotives.

The guard's control panel for the air-doors was only provided on the double-equipped motor cars and the train formation was altered to DM–3T–1T–SM–SM–3T–3T– DM. When trains were operated as 4-car portions the guard remained on the same motor car for both directions of travel. The west-facing single-equipped motor car was provided with First Class accommodation, having been converted from the control trailer car.

The final rehabilitation programme for the 'F' stock came in 1950 with the advent of the 'R' stock on the District. This caused some re-allocation of rolling stock enabling the 1920 stock to be transferred to the Metropolitan line. Because of its speed it was very suitable for working the semi-fast Harrow and Uxbridge services. In addition arrangements were made for 4-car sets to work

SOUTH KENSINGTON
GLOUCESTER ROAD
EARLS COURT
WEST BROMPTON
WALHAM GREEN
PARSONS GREEN
WEST KENSINGTON
BARONS COURT
HAMMERSMITH
RAVENSCOURT PARK
STAMFORD BROOK
TURNHAM GREEN
CHISWICK PARK
ACTON TOWN
EALING COMMON

ST. MARYS
WHITECHAPEL
STEPNEY GREEN
MILE END
BOW ROAD
BROMLEY
WEST HAM
PLAISTOW
UPTON PARK
BARKING
DAGENHAM
HORNCHURCH

SMOKING

the East London shuttle services with the maintenance based on Neasden Depot. The first renovated train went into service on the Metropolitan on 27 February 1951.

At this time the most important work undertaken was the renewal of all the electric power cabling and control wiring, and the installation of the 'A' type electro-pneumatic brake controllers.

Another innovation which has since become standard equipment on the more modern stocks was the provision of mercury-type door interlocks. The door interlock, an

104 *The 'non-stopping' boards and equipment cases on an 'F'-stock motor car* important safety feature provided with air-door installations, ensures that doors are properly closed before the starting signal is given. Until this time these were copper contact 'make and break' switches which required regular cleaning to ensure proper functioning. The mercury switch, having no open contacts and working on the tumble principle, requires little direct attention.

In addition some improvements were made to the bogie springing by the fitting of 12-plate laminated [113]

springs instead of 7-plate. Additional lighting fittings were provided in the car interior to increase the illumination.

The original doors were wood covered with steel panels and these were beyond reasonable repair, so new doors of aluminium alloy were fitted at this time. Although the passenger push-button control was retained and brought into use on the Uxbridge service on which the trains were now running, this equipment was subsequently withdrawn from use. The transfer of this stock released 'P' stock for operating the Circle service which in turn enabled the old Metropolitan Circle stock to be scrapped.

The last 'F' stock passenger train was a 4-car on East London service on Saturday night, 7 September 1963. The last train on the Uxbridge service ran on 15 March 1963.

105 *South Acton shuttle car at South Acton. Unconverted east end of car*

106 *South Acton shuttle car at Acton Town. West end of car converted to provide a driving cab*

28 | 'G' Class— 1923 Stock and the South Acton shuttle

In 1923 it was decided to purchase some new motor cars. The new cars were known as 'G' class and enabled some of the original wooden trailer cars to be scrapped by converting the equivalent number of 1905 motor cars to trailers. The equipments released from the converted motor cars were used to fit out the new cars which were then compatible with the original stock.

A total of 50 car bodies was ordered from the Gloucester Railway Carriage & Wagon Co., together with new motor and trailer trucks. More trucks were ordered than necessary to equip the 50 car bodies so that a number of the original 1905 type bogies which were unsatisfactory could also be replaced. These new bogies were designated 'A2' and 'K2'. The 'A2' motor bogie was of plate-and-angle construction with a 7 ft. 10 in. wheelbase.

The original 'K' bogie was of equalizer bar type with a wheelbase of 5 feet, and this bogie had proved very unreliable, requiring frequent maintenance. The new 'K2' bogie was of plate-and-angle construction, with a wheelbase of 7 ft. 3 in., and 42 of the 1904/5 motor cars were converted to trailers and fitted with 'K2' bogies. These converted cars were at this time designated 'H' class.

It is not now clear where the additional eight sets of equipment came from for the 50 new motor cars as only forty-two 1904/5 motor cars were converted to trailer cars.

In 1925 the rolling stock maintained for general passenger service on the District Railway was stated to be:

	Type	Motor	Trailer	Control Trailer
1904/5	B	147	150	26
Hurst Nelson	C	32	20	—
Metro	D	22	8	—
Gloucester	E	26	4	—
Metro	F	40	48	12
Gloucester	G	50	—	—
Electric Locos.	—	7	—	—
Converted 1904/5	H	—	42	—

Of this total 37 motors and 37 trailers of 'B' class and 8 motors and 8 trailers of 'D' class were owned by the London Midland & Scottish Railway to cover the mileage operated beyond Campbell Road Junction (east of Bow Road station) to Barking, which was controlled by this railway.

When built, 33 of the 'G' class cars were provided facing west and 17 facing east, because by this time the District rolling stock was handed and no turning facilities were provided at Ealing Common Depot for adjusting train make-ups. The only method available for turning cars was to run round the Cromwell Curve triangle, reversing at High Street Kensington and again at South Kensington, or vice versa.

These 'G' class cars were similar in appearance to the earlier District Railway cars, with clerestory roofs and straight-sided bodies. The clerestory roof, however, was carried forward to the end of the carbody and not rounded off as in the American style, and this construction gave the cars a box-like appearance.

The driver was given a totally-enclosed narrow cab across the whole width of the driving end, the practice of providing driving facilities at one end only having now been firmly established as a general operating principle. [115]

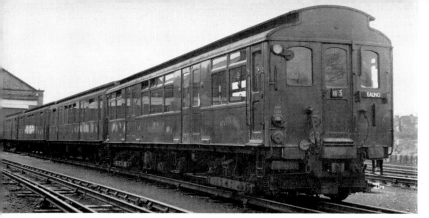

107 *A 4-car 'Q' stock train with a 1923 'G' class westbound motor car leading. The rest of the train consists of two 1935 trailers and an east-end 1927 motor car*

This cab was narrower than that subsequently provided, and in the latter days these cars came to be referred to as 'horse boxes'. In spite of this unpopularity 14 of these survived as 'Q' stock until the withdrawal of the bulk of this class, because such a large proportion were west-facing cars of which only one was required on each District Line train.

On the 'G' class cars the driving cab was unavailable to passengers when not in use by the driver. This facility existed in the older cars, where the driver's controls were locked in a 'cupboard' making it possible for the driver's vestibule to be available for passengers when not required by him. The cab doors were of the hinged type

108 *Interior of 1923 Gloucester car with original grey 'lozenge' moquette*

being locked when not in use. The passenger doors were placed in pairs and were sliding hand-operated, originally being provided with a safety catch and indicator denoting whether the catch was 'locked' or 'unlocked'. This feature was not continued on later stocks.

In 1928, when the first District Line reconstruction programme was undertaken, the 'G' class motor cars had GE69 traction motors and equipment (which was second-hand in any case) removed and replaced by WT54B type traction motors, together with the latest type of BTH electro-magnetic control equipment using an accelerating relay which eliminated hand notching of the controls.

About 10 years later, under the 1935/40 New Works Programme of the London Passenger Transport Board, the 'G' class cars were converted to join the 'Q' stock fleet, being fitted with air-operated doors and electro-pneumatic brakes at Acton Works.

When the 'Q' stock fleet was reduced after the advent of the 'A' stock for the Metropolitan Line in 1960/62 as many 'G' class cars as possible were withdrawn, but 14 west-facing cars had to be retained to provide the 8-car formations which only required one west end motor car.

Although no trailer cars of the 'G' class were originally

109 *A 1923 stock motor car and a wooden 'B' class motor car converted to trailer car with the final numbering scheme*

built, 14 of them ended their days as trailer cars being converted, in 1959, to replace 'Q38' stock trailer cars removed from the 'Q' stock fleet at this time to augment 'OP' and 'R' stock fleets. These 1923 stock cars, however, were among the first to be scrapped in 1962, when the 'Q' stock fleet was reduced upon the introduction of the second batch of 'A' stock on the Metropolitan Line.

Two 1923 stock cars were converted in the 1938 stock reconstruction programme to operate the South Acton shuttle and these were provided with some special features. The two cars chosen for this duty were 4167 and 4176, because of the similarity of the numbering which was easily recognizable by all concerned. The removal of 4176 from the 'Q' stock fleet, however, upset the balance of cars and one east end motor car was turned to west end to compensate, and renumbered.

The South Acton service became a shuttle from Acton Town on 15 February 1932, shortly before the projection of the Piccadilly Line trains west of Hammersmith, which took place on 4 July 1932. Before this a South Acton to Hounslow service had been operated, with the permanent way on the South Acton branch double-

[117]

tracked. This was reduced to a single track on 14 February 1932, when Acton Town station was rebuilt, in anticipation of the Piccadilly extension, with five platforms, one of which was very short and used exclusively as a terminal for the shuttle train to South Acton. A 'B' class motor car No. 37, one of the batch originally built at Lunéville in France, was converted to a double-ended car which could be operated as a single unit. In addition to providing control positions at both ends of the car, two brake cylinders were installed to ensure independent braking of the two bogies to reduce the possibility of a brake failure.

This car was replaced from time to time by a motor car and control trailer of 'B' stock when No. 37 required maintenance.

Originally in the 1935/40 programme it was intended to retain No. 37 on this duty, but the provision of a substitute after the scrapping of the 'B' stock would have presented a problem since all the control trailer cars were also being scrapped. It was decided, therefore, to convert two 1923 stock cars for this duty, one in service and one as standby. The work on these cars included the fitting of duplicate brake cylinders and triple valves and the provision of a driver's cab at both ends. The work which was carried out at Acton Works late in 1939 also included

110 TOP—*K2 bogie*   **111** BOTTOM—*A2 bogie*

the fitting of air-door control but the cars, being intended for one-man operation, had a special interlock circuit which prevented traction control being obtained until the driver had shut himself in the cab. After operating for a number of years with full series-parallel notching, it was considered that this provided too high a speed potential for the short curved track between Acton Town and South Acton, so that an alteration to the control circuit was made, limiting the notching to series only. Because the train service was one-man operated, a pair of emergency telephone wires previously installed only in tunnel sections was erected alongside the shuttle track in 1938. This enabled the driver of the shuttle train to take off the current in an emergency without having to leave his cab.

The South Acton shuttle service ceased to operate on 28 February 1959, and the track has been completely removed. The bridge which carried this line across Bollo Lane was also later removed, so that practically all trace of this service has now disappeared.

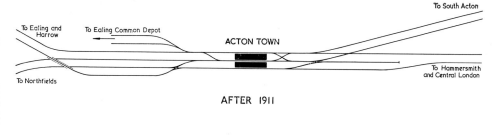

AFTER 1911

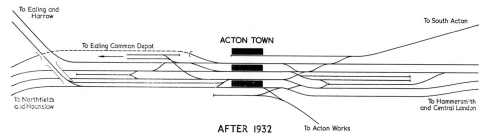

AFTER 1932

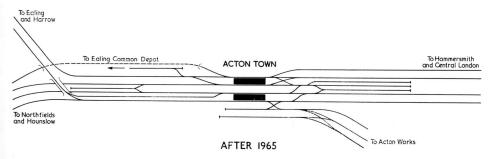

AFTER 1965

112 *Acton Town diagram*

29 | The 1927/31/35 Stock

A complete review of the District Line rolling stock position was undertaken in 1926, and arising from this 101 new cars were ordered from the Birmingham Railway Carriage & Wagon Co.—81 were required as replacements and 20 to provide additional services. As all the cars purchased were motor cars this meant another re-arrangement of the existing fleet, because, at the same time, a total of 263 sets of BTH electro-magnetic equipments, together with their appropriate WT 54B traction motors, were also purchased.

[120]   The rolling stock requirements were set out at this time:

(a) 40M+60T to be provided by 'F' stock incompatible with any other stock.
(b) 263M+248T to be provided by 'standard' BTH stock or 'Main Line' stock as it was then called.
    The 263 motor cars were to be provided as follows: 52 'C' class, 30 'D' class, 30 'E' class, 50 'G' class, 101 'K' class.
(c) 37M+18CT to be provided by stock still equipped with GE69 type traction equipment (but now fitted with GE212 traction motors), known as 'Local' stock.

The provision of this total number of motor cars entailed the conversion of 32 of the 'C', 'D', and 'E' trailer cars to motor cars which had been envisaged in the original design.

The 248 trailer cars required were provided by the 42 'H' class trailers already converted from 1905 motor cars, together with a further 110 similar conversions. The remaining 96 trailer cars required were wooden 'B' class trailer cars fitted with the appropriate through control lines. Apart from 18 control trailers of 'B' class kept to run as 'Local Stock', all the other wooden 'B' class trailers were scrapped. The net result of all this work was to increase the District Line fleet by 42 cars.

The 'Local Stock' was required to operate the shuttle-type services then running from South Acton to Hounslow, and from Acton Town to South Harrow and through to Uxbridge over the Metropolitan Railway tracks.

Of the 101 new cars delivered at this time 91 were delivered complete with bogies, 2 with new trailer bogies only and 8 without any bogies at all. Ten 'A2' type motor bogies and eight 'K2' type trailer bogies were recovered by the conversion of motor cars to trailer cars and the scrapping of some 'B' class cars.

At the end of this programme the District Line had three types of stock in service which were incompatible,

113 *One of the one-hundred-and-one 1927 Birmingham-built motor cars of the 'K' class. This car was for a time owned by the LMS railway as indicated by the M stencilled after the K on the soleplate. This car became car 4315*

because they had different traction control systems using different type traction motors GE 260, WT 54B, and GE 212.

This unfortunate condition continued for over 40 years, providing operating problems which will not entirely be eliminated until the 1980s, and only then if all the replacement stock is compatible.

Externally the 'K' class cars had a less box-like and much smoother appearance than the earlier 'G' class, the corners and lines being rounded off. This improved the look of the cars considerably. The main side lights were made larger and the end of the clerestory was curved down to the cant rail. Four additional seats were provided on the guard's gangway, which could be folded away when not in use. These proved to be rather an obstruction and were later removed.

The five headlights, or marker lights, were enclosed in a single panel on the opposite side of the front of the car to the driver, instead of being exhibited as single lamps distributed widely over the front. The display of the marker lights was controlled by shutters adjusted from inside the cab, instead of movable fan-plates swivelled from the outside.

In addition the destination box placed above the marker light panel was accessible from inside the cab. Previously, destination plates had been inserted externally in frames. These cars were about 49 feet in length overall, slightly longer than previous stock. They were somewhat lighter than the 'G' class, however, weighing about 34 tons compared with 35 tons.

On the earlier stock the guard's gangway had been separated from the car saloon on the trailing end of motor cars by a metal screen. These new cars were provided with a glass draught screen. The guard's door, however, was still of the hinged inward opening type and could not, therefore, be used by passengers when not required by the guard. The car saloon seated 40 passengers and some companion seats were provided. These cars were designated the 'K' class.

About the time of the introduction of this class of stock to District Line service a new type of train-starting equipment was tried, and subsequently adopted, continuing in use until the introduction of air doors. A twin wire arrangement was suspended at car-roof height on the station platforms at the guard's end of the trains. These wires were shorted together by a metal ferrule provided on the end of the guard's green flag handle. This action caused a bell to ring at the driver's end of the platform and for an illuminated S (for start) to appear within the driver's vision.

The 7¾-mile extension to Upminster beyond Barking came into operation on 12 September 1932. The London Midland & Scottish Railway had constructed two additional tracks alongside the old Tilbury & Southend line, so that six stations beyond Barking could be served by District Line trains. A seventh station, Upminster Bridge, was added on 17 December 1934, and an eighth

[121]

114 *A 1931 Feltham motor car with original number. This car was subsequently renumbered*

at Elm Park on 13 May 1935.

In 1931, in anticipation of the additional cars required for the Upminster service, 45 new vehicles designated 'L' class were ordered from the Union Construction Co. of Feltham, a subsidiary company of the Underground group. Of this number only 8 were motor cars, the remaining 37 were trailer cars. The 'L' class motor cars were the first surface stock to be provided with a sliding door at the guard's position.

The trailer cars had the passenger compartment divided into three sections separated by a glazed partition to provide First and Third Class accommodation, and also to divide the First Class into smoking and non-smoking sections. The glazed partitions were provided

115 *Front end of 'B' class motor car not handed. Brake pipe under coupler*

116 *An eastbound 'K' class motor car which is handed*

with swing doors which were returned to the closed position by spring door checks. These trailer cars were of 'lightweight' construction, since complete with bogies they weighed only 23 tons although constructed of steel.

The bogies for the cars were built by Metropolitan-Cammell, the electrical control equipment by BTH, and the WT 54B motors by G.E.C. to match the equipments obtained for the 1927/28 conversion programme. The traction motors for these cars, however, were delivered with roller bearings, while the earlier motors of this type had to undergo a conversion programme at Acton Works to change from white metal to roller bearings. This change was one of the major labour-saving innovations at this time. Before the advent of roller bearings on the traction motors, oiling of the motor bearings had to be undertaken at least once a week. Now, with the introduction of grease-lubricated roller bearings, the period was extended first to 3 months and later to 12 months, while today consideration is being given to even longer periods between lubrication of this equipment.

All eight motor cars of this class faced west, but the service requirements at this time needed the addition of six eastbound cars and only two westbound. To balance the stock requirements, therefore, six of the 1910 'C' class were turned at Acton Works from west to east. The physical turning was, of course, arranged round Cromwell Curve, but the work at Acton consisted of changing control connections and air lines for coupling purposes and other minor equipment alterations.

These eight 'L' class motor cars were, in fact, owned by the London, Midland & Scottish Railway, as the mileage operated arising out of the extension to Upminster called for an increase in its ownership of vehicles. The total ownership by the LMS was raised at this time to 57 motor cars and 53 trailer cars, or the equivalent of 13 trains plus a few spare cars. However, these cars were never specially worked together, and no distinction was made as to their operating routes. For operating purposes

[123]

117 *Interior of 'M' class car, showing the partition and door provided for the division of First Class accommodation into smoking and non-smoking*

118 *A 6-car train of 1935 stock fitted with air doors outside Hammersmith (Met.) station*

they were part of the District fleet and the ownership arrangements were purely financial. Nationalization in 1948 removed the necessity for any joint ownership of rolling stock.

The London Passenger Transport Board's creation in 1933 had the effect of amalgamating the Metropolitan and District Railways, and some consolidation of the services provided was inevitable. One of the first effects of this was the projection of Metropolitan trains to Barking, and this service was at first provided from Uxbridge but later by the extension of the Hammersmith & City service from Whitechapel. This improved the frequency of the services over this section in addition to providing a route to the north of the City from the East End without the need to change.

In order to obtain some new vehicles quickly it was decided to repeat the design which was available. Orders were placed for 28 cars, 14 motors and 14 trailers from the Birmingham Railway Carriage & Wagon Co., and a further 26 trailer cars from Metro-Cammell. Although the designs were almost identical and similar to the 'L' class, the 28 cars were given the classification 'M' and the Metro-Cammell cars the class letter 'N'.

Out of the 40 trailer cars built, only 5 were plain Third Class trailers, the other 35 were composites, identical with the 'L' class, having three sections with glazed partitions.

The Birmingham cars were actually delivered in four complete 6-car train sets and operated for a few years in block formations, being the first District Line type trains (with the exception of the 'F' stock) since the original electrification to do so. The reason for this arrangement arose from the fact that this group of cars was fitted with electro-pneumatic brakes and air-operated doors. In fact these were the first surface stock trains to enter service with air-door equipment. The cars were equipped at this time with passenger-operated door buttons so that only those doors through which the passengers wished to board or alight were opened. This was the first use of this equipment on Underground trains. The trains went into service on the Hammersmith & City Line, providing the extra operating trains required for the extension of this service to Barking. Some trains worked from the H. & C. Line to East Ham from 30 March 1936, but when First Class accommodation was withdrawn from the Hammersmith & City and East London Line service on 4 May 1936, eight trains an hour out of the twelve provided at the peak periods began working through to Whitechapel and Barking. The provision of First Class accommodation on the new trailer cars was, therefore, short-lived, although this class was reinstated when these cars were later transferred to the District Line. On 1 February 1940 First Class accommodation was withdrawn except to Aylesbury and the Watford Joint Lines, where it survived until 6 October 1941.

When the cars were transferred to the District the electro-pneumatic brake had to be temporarily disconnected and the doors converted to hand operation, because at this time it was necessary for the trailer cars to work with the 1910/13 motor cars which were not suitable for conversion to air-doors.

There were originally 112 motor cars of 1910/13 stock retained in 1938 and, together with seventy-seven 1931/35 stock trailer cars, they formed the 'H' class stock. This was the second use of the letter 'H', as none of the original 'H' stock trailer cars were now left. 'H' now stood for 'hand-worked' door stock.

119 *'R' stock with passenger open-door control*

Of the 112 original motor cars, one had been damaged beyond repair in the Charing Cross collision in May 1938, and during 1938/39 fourteen were converted to trailer cars, so that the fleet of 'H' stock became 97 motor cars and 91 trailer cars. All this work, however, formed part of the 'Q' stock programme which began in 1937 and was not completed when the Second World War broke out in 1939.

ORIGINAL NUMBER GROUPINGS OF 'O', 'P', & 'Q' STOCK AS DELIVERED

Reference No.	Description of Stock	Car Builders	Number of Vehicles	'A' Cars Numbers	Number of Vehicles	'D' Cars Numbers
1 1A	'O' stock Motors	B G	29 29	13000–13028 13029–13057	29 29	14000–14028 14029–14057
2	3rd Class 'O' stock Trailers	G	20	013058–013077	19	014058–014076
3	1st & 3rd Class 'O' stock Trailers	G	9	013078–013086	10	014077–014086
4	1st & 3rd Class 'P' stock Trailers	G	15	013087–013101	14	014087–014100
5	3rd Class 'Q' stock Trailers	G	3	013102–013104	3	014101–014103
6	1st & 3rd Class 'Q' stock Trailers	G	62	013105–013166	63	014104–014166
7	3rd Class 'Q' stock Trailers	G	26	013167–013192	26	014167–014192
8	'P' stock Motors	G	53	13193–13245	53	14193–14245
9	'P' stock Motors	B	12	13246–13257	12	14246–14257
10	1st & 3rd Class 'P' stock Trailers	B	4	013258–013261	4	014258–014261
11 11A	'P' stock Motors	B B	2 6	13262–13263 13264–13269	8	14262–14269
12	1st & 3rd Class 'P' stock Trailers	B	4	013270–013273	4	014270–014273
13	'Q' stock Motors	G	10	4402–4420	15	4409–4437
				(Even Nos. only)		(Odd Nos. only)
Total			**284**	**573**	**289**	

B = Birmingham Railway Carriage & Wagon Co. Ltd.   G = Gloucester Railway Carriage & Wagon Co. Ltd.

30 | The 'O', 'P', and 'Q' Stock family

For the new surface rolling stock construction under the 1935/40 New Works Programme modernization scheme 573 cars were purchased. All these vehicles were built by two carbuilders: the Gloucester Railway Carriage & Wagon Co. and the Birmingham Railway Carriage & Wagon Co. between 1936 and 1940 and consisted of three different classes—the 'O', 'P', and 'Q' stock. Basically all the cars were similar in general construction and the trailer cars were so built that they could be converted into motor cars at a later date if necessary.

The original order covered the purchase of rolling stock to replace the Hammersmith & City trains and consisted of 116 cars, all motor cars, equally divided between the two carbuilders and to be formed into two-car units. These were original 'O' stock. The stock ordered to replace the Metropolitan car stock was designated the 'P' stock, and that required for the District replacement arrangements the 'Q' stock. There were a number of alterations to the original orders, but the opposite table shows the number groupings of the cars concerned as delivered, but not necessarily the order in which they entered service. In order to clarify the story the reference numbers used in this table will be referred to in the text as required.

The 'O' stock (Ref. 1 and 1A) at the ordering stage were known as the Hammersmith & City Replacement Stock and, as they were designed to operate in 2-car units, the 116 cars could be made up into 19×6-car trains with

one 2-car unit spare. Together with 4×6-car trains of 1935 stock already operating on this service, this made a total of 23×6-car trains which equalled the number of old stock previously required to provide the Hammersmith service, including maintenance spares.

This new stock was different in appearance from any which had previously been built. Each carbody was just over 51 feet long and, apart from the equipment fitted to the underframe, each car of the pair was in general layout a mirror image of the other. Each car was provided with one single and two double passenger doors down each side in the passenger saloon, and because these cars were built for the Hammersmith & City service only one class of travel was now provided. As originally built the 'A' end motor cars were virtually divided into two compartments [127]

120 *'CP' stock with altered tripcock resetting cord*

by glass partitions, reaching full body height but without a swing door providing smoking and non-smoking space. No door division was provided because the double glass partition which formed the air intake for equipment cooling made a natural division of the car. This air intake ventilated the interior of the vehicle and also provided clean air for cooling the metadyne machine (described later) carried on the 'A' car.

Each carbody had seats for 40 passengers with, in addition, two tip-up seats provided on the trailing end bulkheads. The sliding doors were pneumatically operated and when built were fitted with passenger door control. The push-buttons were fitted to the body door pillars and not on the door frames themselves as arranged on the original 1935 stock fitted with this equipment.

The guard's door controls for these air-operated doors were placed in the driver's cab because the guard on Hammersmith & City stock had always worked from the rear cab, and at the time of placing the orders for the stock this practice was continued.

The 'O' stock cars were fitted originally with semi-loose cushions covered with moquette, but these were later converted to standard interior sprung seats fitted to subsequent vehicles.

Externally the car windows were flush with the body. This was effected by the use of rebated glass. The side panels were flared out at the bottom and the lower end of the sliding doors followed this contour. This was done to take the place of the side running boards provided on the earlier stocks and avoided having gaps at platforms. It was useful to avoid providing running boards with air-door stock because of the hazard if foolhardy passengers hung on to the outside after the train started with the doors closed. This arrangement gave the cars a very pleasing appearance, which was spoiled as far as the

'Q' stock was concerned by the need to operate some formations with stock of new and old designs.

In addition to the original 116 cars of 'O' stock a further 457 cars were ordered from the same carbuilders, making a total of 573 vehicles of which 287 were motor cars. All except 25 of these motor cars were provided with metadyne equipment and formed into 2- or 3-car units. The 3-car units included a trailer car. The cars of the units were close-coupled, with a bar coupling not normally disconnected. The units themselves were made up into train sets of 4-, 5-, 6-, 7-, or 8-car lengths by coupling appropriate combinations of 2- and 3-car units together by means of a Wedglock automatic coupler which coupled them together pneumatically, electrically and mechanically.

The second batch of metadyne-controlled vehicles was designated 'P' stock and these had a similar external appearance, but were different from the 'O' stock cars in several respects.

The door controls operated by the guard were provided on the 'P' stock in the then conventional tube stock position at the end gangway of the motor car. The metadyne cooling intake provided in the 'A', or west end, cars on 'P' stock was placed under the middle companion seats without the provision of a glass partition.

Some 'O' stock cars were subsequently fitted with centre grab poles in the middle of the double-door gangways to provide additional support for standing passengers. This feature lasted for several years, but was later removed because the pole in the middle of this standing area proved to be an obstruction tending to restrict the free flow of passengers under crowded conditions.

The bogies were of welded steel plate construction and were asymmetric in design, that is—the axles were un-

121 ABOVE—*Interior of 'O' stock D car*   **122** BELOW—*Interior of 'O' stock A car, showing the glass partition provided for the metadyne air intake, between the centre bay slats*

equally spaced about the pivot point. The axle nearer the centre carried the single traction motor fitted to each motor bogie. In this way a greater proportion of the car weight was available for adhesion. The bogie was designed for good riding qualities, having the bolster springing and the swing links placed as far apart as possible. The wheels were 36 inches in diameter with full-sized tyres and the gear ratio provided was 16/65. The motor axle had a roller bearing sleeve on which the MV145AZ type traction motor was mounted. All previous surface rolling stock had been provided with plain white metal bearings for mounting axle-hung traction motors on the axle. The wheels were fitted with either SKF or Hoffman parallel roller-type axle boxes, a feature of this type of axle box being the ease of removal from the axle journal.

The trailer bogies were almost identical with the motor bogies but did not carry a traction motor and, therefore, neither axle had a suspension sleeve. Two brake cylinders were provided, one which actuated the brake blocks on the motored wheels or their equivalent on a trailer bogie, and the other on the trailer wheels. This arrangement enabled a differential braking system to be installed in connection with the metadyne control which included the provision of regenerative braking.

Each 2- or 3-car unit of 'O' and 'P' stock was fitted with one compressor and one 5 kw. motor-generator set which provided a 50-volt DC supply for control and lighting. The lighting was provided by incandescent bulbs along each side of the roof line, and the bulbs were originally covered by shovel-type lamp shades. These shades were removed in later years when a higher lighting standard was considered necessary, and un-shaded antiglare-type bulbs were fitted to provide an increase in the illumination.

The cars of similar construction for the District Line services were known as 'Q' stock and, with the exception of 25 motor cars, were all trailer cars. These cars had to work with existing older rolling stock not equipped with 50-volt lighting circuits. The interior appearance was the same but the lamps were energized from a 600-volt supply having five lamps in series. The shades were not removed from these cars as a safety measure, in case unauthorized persons tampered with the lamps in these high-voltage circuits.

Out of the total of 573 cars, 286 were trailer cars. They were constructed so that they could, in fact, be converted to motor cars, because it was considered that at some time in the future—after the improvements to the power supply had been completed—a higher performance would be required from the rolling stock in the way of acceleration, and this could only be met by increasing the number of motored axles on the trains. The cars were built 'handed'. Provision was made for a driving cab at either the 'A' or 'D' end in equal numbers. The numbering system adopted shows the arrangement. At the position where the driving cab would be provided the cab door of the hinged type was fitted but sealed up, and the four extra seats in trailer cars were provided against the car end. The end corridor door at this position was not provided with a droplight as it was the equivalent of a driver's leading cab door.

Although only a few of these trailer cars were converted to 'P' stock motor cars, advantage was taken of this provision when the 'R' stock was subsequently purchased.

31 'Q' Stock

In 1938 work began rehabilitating the District Line rolling stock built from 1923 onwards. This included the provision of pneumatically-operated doors, the fitting of electro-pneumatic brakes together with retardation control, and a number of other minor alterations. The stock retained the 600-volt power bus line which ran from end to end of the train, connecting all the collector shoes together and retained the electro-magnetic traction control gear operating with WT54B type traction motors.

The 1910/13 motor cars were not suitable for conversion. These cars were, therefore, retained as hand-worked door stock working with more modern trailer cars. There were originally a total of 112 motor cars of 1910/13 vintage, but there were only 77 modern trailer cars of 1931/35 types. The 112 motor cars were reduced by 15, one being damaged beyond economical repair in a collision at Charing Cross in May 1938, and 14 being converted to trailer cars to augment the seventy-seven 1931/35 types to form an equitable balance of hand-worked door stock. This stock which later became known as 'H' class (for hand-worked doors) was made up with an equal number of motors and trailers into 6-car trains, the formation being M–T–T–M–T–M with the 4-car portion at the west end of the train.

At this time some of the more modern trailers which had been operating on the Hammersmith & City service had the air-door equipment removed, the doors converted to hand-operation and the electro-pneumatic brake equipment disconnected, because the hand-worked door stock was only provided with the Westinghouse air brake.

The 77 more modern trailer cars were, of course, fitted or re-equipped with electro-pneumatic brakes and air-doors when the 'R' stock rolling stock programme was begun after the end of the Second World War, and the other hand-worked door cars were scrapped. The advent of the 'R' stock programme enabled the older 1910/13 cars to be scrapped, but 3 × 6-car trains were retained composed entirely of 1910/13 cars to work the Olympia shuttle service. However, these trains were considered to be very poor advertisements for Britain, and, of course, for London Transport, when International Exhibitions were in session at Olympia, and they were rarely used for this purpose. So the need for their retention disappeared and the last of the pre-First World War District stock was scrapped.

Confining all the modern trailer cars to work with the 1910/13 motor cars meant that a new fleet of trailer cars had to be purchased to run with 173 motor cars of 1923, 1927, 1931 and 1935 vintage after their conversion to electro-pneumatic brakes and pneumatic doors. A total of 183 trailer cars similar in design to the 'OP' stock were provided (Ref. 5, 6 and 7). In addition 25 new motor cars (Ref. 13) were also provided. This new stock was given the designation 'Q' and all the fleet, when converted to air-doors, eventually became known as 'Q' stock.

Fifteen of these new motor cars were given secondhand electrical equipment salvaged from the fourteen 1910/13 cars converted to trailer cars and the one which had been scrapped. At this time, therefore, only ten new equipments of the old-fashioned electro-magnetic type were in fact purchased.

The first 'Q' stock train, consisting of converted motor cars and new trailer cars with pneumatic doors and electro-pneumatic brakes, entered service on the District Line in November 1938.

The 'Q' stock 8-car train formation was:

$$M–T–T–M \times T–M \times T–M$$
$$1–2–3–4 \times 5–6 \times 7–8$$

The air-doors included the 'passenger open' feature which allowed the passengers at certain stations to open individual pairs of doors without the whole of the doors on the side of the train being opened. This feature was discontinued during the black-out imposed by the Second World War, and was never fully restored on the District Line.

This train formation required one 'A' end motor car and three 'D' end motor cars in positions 4, 6, and 8. All these cars were Third Class, but of the 183 new trailer cars purchased 125 were composite (Ref. 6) providing three sections, First Class smoking and non-smoking at one end, and the remaining half of the car Third Class. Composite trailer cars were provided in positions 3, 5, and

123 *The original passenger door control fitted to the 1935 stock. The 'Push to Open' sign was illuminated when the door circuit was alive*

7 in the train formation. Only position 2 was a full Third Class car.

Another formation problem beset the 'Q' stock after operation commenced. This arose from the practice of uncoupling the 8-car trains to 6 cars for the off-peak running. The two cars, known as east end portions, placed in the 7 and 8 positions, had to be shunted over considerable distances during coupling or uncoupling with the trailer car leading. Some special fittings including emergency brake handles and grab poles for the use of the shunter had to be installed on these trailer cars, which were then confined to the No. 7 position in the train formation.

At this time the District Line train operation required a service of 47×6-car and 37×8-car trains. Eleven of the 8-car trains were normally provided by 'F' (1920) stock and 27 of the 6-car formations by hand-worked door stock. The remainder of the 6- and 8-car formations, the latter being those which uncoupled, were made up of 'Q' stock. This was the general arrangement during the war years 1939/45. The hand-worked door stock was restricted to the minimum of duties, especially under black-out conditions, as this door arrangement mixed with air-operated door trains was thought to be dangerous. After the war the introduction of the 'R' stock enabled the hand-worked door stock to be withdrawn from service and the 'F' stock to be transferred to the Metropolitan Line. The District train service was then provided by 'Q' and 'R' stock.

The 'R' stock programme utilized the original conception of the 'OPQ' family of cars in that all the trailer cars could be converted to motor cars. In the first batch of 'R' stock, therefore, a total of 82 'Q' stock trailer cars were converted to driving motor cars, and their place in the 'Q' stock trains was taken by the conversion of the

seventy-seven 1931/35 stock trailer cars to pneumatic doors and electro-pneumatic brakes. This substitution naturally resulted in an unbalance of motor cars, so that to match the trailer car position the eight Feltham-built 1931 stock motor cars and the 14 Birmingham-built 1935 stock motor cars were converted to trailer cars. This, in turn, upset the balance of east and west facing cars so that, in addition, seven 1927 motor cars were turned from east to west.

This conversion work was not completed until 1955 and for a time a number of motor cars ran in trailer positions with the control equipment rendered inoperative. To distinguish these cars from driving motor cars they appeared with a 'o' prefix to the 4xxx number. At the same time the 8xxx numbered trailer cars were operating in both 'H' class and 'Q' class trains. Those converted for working 'Q' class trains had the numbers also prefixed with a cipher.

By 1951 there were only six 6-car trains of 'H' class operating in service, and this was finally reduced to two retained for a few years for the Olympia shuttle service. The trailer cars were obtained by converting some 1910/13 motor cars to trailers as all the more modern trailer cars had by this time been converted to operate in 'Q' stock trains.

The second batch of 'R' stock took a further 43 'Q' stock trailers and then, in 1959, a further 7 were required. Another 17 'Q' stock trailers were modified to become 'OP' stock for lengthening the Circle trains from 5 to 6 cars. This again upset the balance of motor to trailers in the 'Q' stock fleet, and fourteen 1923 stock motor cars were now converted to trailer cars. This work was completed by January 1960.

A further depletion of 'Q' stock trailers then took place, a total of 13 being required to ensure that all the remaining

'CP' stock 2-car units released from the Metropolitan Line on the introduction of the 'A' stock were built up to 3-car units. The transfer of these 'CP' stock trains to the District Line then enabled the scrapping of the 'Q' stock to commence.

In the first phase of the 'Q' stock displacement as many of the 1923 stock cars as possible were scrapped, but to retain the balance of east and west end cars without the necessity to turn further motor cars, 14 of these older vehicles at the 'A' or west end of the trains were retained.

The advent of the 'C69' stock now being introduced into service will enable the 'Q' stock to be scrapped, but 28 cars have been earmarked for the East London service. These 28 cars will be made up into 7 × 4-car units, utilizing 14 of the 25 'Q' type motor cars and 14 of 'Q' trailer cars. The cars concerned have been given a reconditioning overhaul at Acton Works. An additional hand brake has been fitted to the 'D' motor cars to ensure an adequate parking brake if these units have to be held on an incline.

32 | The Metadyne Stock—subsequently 'CO/CP' Stock

At the time that new stock was being considered for Metropolitan and District Line replacement requirements a new system of control was being developed by Metropolitan Vickers known as the metadyne system. Arrangements were made in 1934 for a 6-car experimental train to be tested to see whether this system could be applied to the new rolling stock to be purchased.

The six cars chosen for this experiment were old Metropolitan motor cars built between 1904 and 1907. The cars were converted at Acton Works during 1934, being fitted with metadyne traction control equipments and externally finished in a red and cream livery similar to that applied to the reconditioned Circle cars.

The metadyne system involved the provision of a rotary transformer (metadyne means 'conversion of power') placed between the line supply and the traction motors. This machine was able to supply four traction motors and in order to conform to the accepted practice of having only two traction motors to each car the experimental cars were converted in pairs. One carried the metadyne machine and control gear and the other was provided with the auxiliary equipment which included a motor generator set to supply low voltage for control and lighting.

Two traction motors on each car were supplied from one metadyne machine so that the cars could not be worked singly and always worked in pairs. Each pair of cars could be operated separately having a driving position at the outer ends. Test trains could, therefore, either be worked in 2-, 4- or 6-car formations. When this test train had completed its trials the metadyne equipment was removed and fitted to three battery locomotives which are still in service, but the cars were scrapped.

The metadyne system was attractive for several reasons:

(1) one set of control equipment could control two motor cars;

(2) the system was inherently regenerative so that an economical braking system could be developed;

(3) no starting resistances were needed and the acceleration was smooth.

As a result of the tests carried out during 1935 and 1936 over practically all the electrified tracks of the Metropolitan and District lines, and later tests in passenger service, it was decided to equip most of the new stock with metadyne control.

The first batch was the 'O' stock consisting of 116 cars made up into 58 two-car units. The 'O' stock, however, did not go into service immediately on the Hammersmith Line, the first experimental service being between High Street, Kensington, and Putney Bridge with a 4-car unit on 13 September 1937. The first 6-car train composed of three 2-car units went into service on the Hammersmith Line in January 1938.

Technical problems arose, however, with the maximum demand and the effect of regeneration with a train entirely composed of motor cars, and it was decided to dilute the train formation by the insertion of trailer cars into the units. To do this 58 trailer cars (Ref. 2 & 3) were ordered from the Gloucester Co. to make each of the 2-car units into a 3-car set. The problem was virtually one of timing as it was considered that sometime in the future trains composed all of motor cars would be necessary to meet the traffic demands, and these trailer cars were designed in such a way that they could easily be converted into motor cars at a future date.

The second batch of cars, designated 'P' stock, was required for replacement of all the car stock on the Metropolitan Line, where 8-car formations as well as 6-car formations were required. It was, therefore, decided to adopt the formation

$$M–T–M \times M–T–M \times M–M$$

that is, an 8-car train made up of two 3-car and one 2-car units. The units were close coupled with automatic couplers at the outer ends. The automatic couplers provided were similar to those adopted for the 1938 Tube stock ordered at the same time, providing mechanical, electrical, and pneumatic coupling.

The 'O' and 'P' stock were compatible both as to control and coupling arrangements but there were a number of fundamental differences so that equipment itself was not interchangeable. In particular the metadyne machines were not interchangeable. This machine, which weighed about 3 tons, consisted of three rotating machines known as the exciter, the regulator, and the metadyne machine itself, mechanically coupled together. [135]

124 *The handgrab development of the 'Surface' stock*

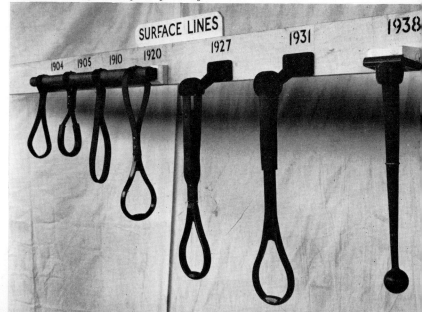

The electrical connections of the machines were different so that they were not interchangeable between 'O' and 'P' stock cars. This was a serious disadvantage in later years when a spate of major defects requiring extensive repairs arose. This epidemic was one of the reasons why consideration was given to the withdrawal and replacement of the equipment. Some spare 1938 Tube stock PCM equipments were available at the time, and as the arrangements for which they had been purchased had not yet matured because the operation of this equipment had exceeded all expectations in reliability, it was decided to convert one metadyne train operating on the Circle Line service to PCM control. This, in the first instance, provided additional metadyne spares for metadyne equipments by cannibalization, but in addition enabled the conversion costs to be assessed.

The first converted train, which became known as 'CO/CP' stock as it contained both 'O' and 'P' stock cars, went into service on the Circle on 31 March 1955 and subsequently all the 'O' and 'P' stock was converted.

Another difference of a fundamental nature between 'O' and 'P' stock was the operating position of the guard. In 'O' stock the door control boxes were provided in the driver's cab so that the guard worked from the extreme rear of the train, which conformed to the previous operating practice of the Hammersmith & City Line with hand-operated doors. The 'P' stock, however, had the door control boxes placed on the end gangway conforming with previous Underground practice where air-doors were fitted.

With the introduction of trailer cars into the 'O' stock 2-car units, 19 units were released from H. & C. service for operation elsewhere. Apart from the Hammersmith & City services, the requirements for the Metropolitan Line at this time could be fulfilled by the provision of 64×3-car and 28×2-car units. The problem which then had to be overcome was that the 'O' stock units could not be operated at the end of 8-car trains in the central area platforms because of the length limitation which would leave the rear end cab in the tunnel with the guard unsighted for his platform duties.

Subsequent adjustments to the stock allocation made it necessary to purchase 73 'P' stock units which, together with the 19 units of 'O' stock, made the total of 92 units required. As 28 of these were to be of 2-car formation without trailer cars, it was arranged that the A-end 'O' stock cars (those numbered from 13XXX) were placed at the west end of 19 of these units; these would then

[136]

125 *The first Gloucester-built 2-car unit of 'O' stock at Ealing Common. The leading car carried the metadyne machine*

normally be attached to the east end of 6-car formations to make 8-car trains. Having placed these cars in a position where the door control equipment was virtually unused, it was then further arranged that six of the new motor cars of 'P' stock (Ref. 11A) which would also be A-end cars should not be provided with door control boxes. The decision to have six of these cars without door boxes instead of nine arose because the service requirement was 25 × 8-car trains, not 28 trains, so that the remaining three units were spares. In theory, therefore, the provision of door boxes enabled these cars to be utilized as spares for either type of operation. This theoretical decision was not, in fact, very helpful in practice, because splitting of any unit which was bar-coupled to change from a 2- to 3-car was an engineering operation not achieved by a simple shunting process. These cars without guard's control panels were coded 'P1'.

The D-end 'O' stock cars (those numbered from 14xxx) were placed in 3-car units and were only at the ends of 6-car formations, and could be accommodated at all the stations where such formations were operated.

The effect of this programme was disastrous to the carefully prepared numbering scheme which had been devised to pair the 'A' and 'D' motor cars with the 13xxx and 14xxx numbers matching, and thereby simplify the recording requirements.

The 'O' formations operated as 6-car sets and provided the Hammersmith & City service to Whitechapel and Barking, while the mixed 'O' and 'P' stock maintained mainly the Metropolitan Line's Uxbridge service until the introduction of 'R' stock enabled the old Circle stock to be replaced by a re-arrangement of duties of 'F' stock and 'OP' stock.

The transfer of 'F' stock to the Uxbridge service enabled 'OP' stock units to be released to make up 5-car sets composed of one 3-car and one 2-car unit to take over the Circle workings. The first 5-car 'P' stock train began operating on the Circle service in February 1947, but it was nearly four years before the complete service was provided by this stock. Although it was hoped that this change in the rolling stock would improve the reliability of the service, this was only marginally satisfactory. The Circle service is particularly arduous, each train making journeys of over 350 miles each day, and starting and stopping every half mile. This began to take its toll of the metadyne equipment, and the decision was then made to convert the trains working the Circle service to 'PCM' control.

The first converted train began working on 30 April 1956 and after conversion the first digit of the car number of the motor cars was altered from '1' to '5', so that the A-end cars became 53xxx and the D cars 54xxx.

Subsequently 17 × 5-car trains were converted allowing only three spare trains against four previously held. This [137]

126 *A 5-car 'P' stock on Circle service*

indicated to some extent the measure of the improvement of reliability which it was expected to be gained by the conversion. These spare trains, however, were now confined to Circle workings and did not form part of a greater fleet which could be used on the Metropolitan Main Line, where other 'O/P' stock still operated. Improved reliability was in fact achieved so that it was decided to convert all the 'O/P' stock to 'PCM' in two stages, first the Hammersmith & City fleet and then the Metropolitan main-line fleet. This latter conversion was arranged to coincide with the release of the 'P' stock for transfer to the District Line upon the introduction of the second batch of 'A' stock (the 'A62' cars).

The 5-car Circle trains were overcrowded in comparison with the District and Hammersmith & City 6-car trains so that it was then decided to increase the train length by the insertion of a trailer car into the 2-car unit. The transfer of 'P' stock to the District service enabled some of the 'Q' stock trains to be replaced and the fleet reduced. Seventeen 'Q' stock trailer cars were, therefore, converted to work as 'CP' trailers. The conversion involved the alteration of the lighting from the 600-volt series to the 50-volt parallel arrangement, and the couplings from Ward to bar. The work of converting these cars was carried out at Acton Works during 1959/60. The first 6-car train operated on the Circle service on 15 June 1959.

The lengthening of the Circle trains to six cars and the conversion of the H. & C. trains to 'PCM' made it possible to integrate these two services so that the maintenance of all the 'CO/CP' stock working Metropolitan services was concentrated at Hammersmith, enabling Neasden to concentrate on the enlarged 'A' stock fleet. When the Metropolitan 'P' stock fleet was first released for working on the District Line only 6-car formations

were required because the 'R' stock at that time could provide all the necessary 8-car workings.

As there were still 12×2-car units involved in the transfer it was necessary to increase these to 3-car formation and a further 12 'Q' stock trailers were converted to 'CP' stock during 1961/62. Subsequently, after the introduction of the 'C69' stock to Hammersmith and Circle workings and the transfer of all 'CO/CP' stock to the District, 8-car workings will again be required and a number of trailer cars will then be scrapped to create 2-car units again. These 2-car units will have the 'CO' stock cars at the west end because of the old problem of the guard's position.

The train formation will again be:
$$M-T-M \times M-T-M \times M-M$$
$$1-2-3 \times 4-5-6 \times 7-8$$
so that the A-end 'CO' stock cars will always occupy No. 7 position while the D-ends will be placed in either No. 3 or No. 6. This change will not be completed until all the 'C69' stock has entered service in 1971.

The 'OP' stock fleet suffered badly due to war damage. At the end of the war the fleet was short of two 'A' or west end cars and five 'D' or east end cars, so that in order to restore the balance three 'P' stock trailer cars were converted to D-end 'P' stock motor cars by the Gloucester Railway Carriage & Wagon Co. at the same time as the 'R' stock was being built.

One other interesting conversion was undertaken during the war when car No. 14233, which had been severely damaged in an air raid on 18 September 1940, was repaired by using half of another car, 'Q' stock trailer No. 013167 damaged at a later time. For a number of years after this car was returned to service on 29 September 1941, it carried a card with photographs showing the work involved.

33 | 'R' Stock

At the end of the Second World War it was felt desirable to withdraw all the hand-worked door stock, so the Circle stock and the District 'C', 'D', and 'E' had to be replaced.

New stock which was designated 'R' was ordered for the District. The initial delivery was intended to replace the hand-worked door District cars, and subsequently in addition to enable the 'F' stock to be transferred to the Metropolitan Line. This transfer in turn enabled the hand-operated door stock on the Circle service to be replaced.

The new trains of 'R' stock were composed entirely of motor cars but the general design of the bodywork was similar to the 'P' stock. This design feature made it possible to convert existing 'Q' stock trailer cars to motor cars as had been envisaged in the original arrangements when they were purchased.

All but six of the driving motor cars, therefore, were obtained by converting the appropriate handed 'Q' stock trailers to driving motor cars. This conversion work was mainly undertaken by the Gloucester Railway Carriage & Wagon Co., although, at the end of the 'R' stock programme, some were converted at Acton Works. The newly-built cars of the first batch were designated 'R47' stock and were all non-driving motor cars. They were built by both the Gloucester and Birmingham Carriage Companies. The use of non-driving motor cars in the train formations on Surface rolling stock was a new departure copied from the Tube stock arrangement introduced in 1938. Although all the cars in the trains were motor cars, only 50% of the axles were in fact motored. Only one traction motor was carried on each bogie, continuing the practice of the 'OPQ' family of cars. The bogie itself was again asymmetric, with a greater proportion of the weight on the axle carrying the traction motor. The new bogies were, however, of a new design, incorporating side frames of all-welded construction but with the transverse members riveted to them to provide some flexing, the absence of which in the earlier designs had produced cracking of side members from time to time. Individual brake cylinders for each brake block were provided similar to the practice established for Tube stock cars, but the converted cars retained the metadyne

[139]

127 *'R' stock showing guard's control panels*

arrangement, having two brake cylinders mounted on the bogie, one applying pressure to the trailer wheels and the other to the motor wheels. This was arranged to avoid any major modification to these bogies.

The trains of 'R' stock were designed to be operated in only two formations, six or eight cars, with the ability to uncouple an 8-car set to form a 6-car. This followed the District Line operating practice at that time with 'Q' stock trains.

In order to economize in driving positions and keep to a minimum the 'Q' stock trailer cars to be converted to motor cars, the train formation provided was the most inflexible yet devised. Each car in a 6-car formation had a specific position with the last two cars repeating to form an 8-car train. The 8-car train formation was:

$$1–2–3–4 \times 5–6 \times 5–6$$

with car No. 1 being an A-end driving motor car and the two type 6 cars being D-end driving motor cars, and nearly all cars of this type were rebuilt 'Q' trailer cars of 1938 vintage.

One of the problems at this time was releasing sufficient cars for this work to be undertaken, as there were no additional trains available at the beginning to provide a working float. The position did improve when 'R' stock trains began operating in service, but the inflexible

128 RIGHT—*View of 'R' stock driver's cab*

129 BELOW—*'R' stock motor bogie with the original frame which had shoegear*

130 *'R' stock train at Upminster Depot yard. This is an R59 train with red lining, later removed. The leading motor car is an R38/3 car painted aluminium to match the unpainted R59 cars*

train formation made up with cars from different car-builders also caused serious difficulties. At one particular time in the programme there were as many as 40 'R' stock cars delivered in London but it was not possible to make up a single 'R' stock train because one particular type of car was missing.

The conversion work consisted of fitting a driver's cab where provision had already been made for it, thereby reducing the seating capacity from 44 to 40, and the fitting of door control boxes with appropriate wiring at the other end for the guard. The lighting arrangements now provided consisted of two-foot fluorescent tubes placed along the car lines of the roof eliminating the

600-volt series wiring from the 'Q' stock trailers. It was the first batch of Underground rolling stock to be delivered that had been fitted throughout with fluorescent lighting. A total of 24 tubes was provided in each car, supplied in parallel circuits from a 110-volt AC supply obtained from a motor generator set. This motor generator set (a 600-volt/50-volt DC converter) had, in addition to the 50-volt DC winding for control and emergency battery charging, an auxiliary winding on the pole faces. This winding generated the 110-volt AC supply at a frequency of 850 cycles, which powered the fluorescent lighting. At the ends of cars inside the saloon, some battery-fed tungsten lamps were provided which acted as an emergency lighting supply in case the motor generator failed. The motor generator set was fitted to four cars out of the eight on a full-length train,

[141]

in positions 1, 4, and 6, and proved to be very reliable in operation, but unfortunately the ac winding produced a high-pitched humming noise which made the machine undesirable for tube working, and this arrangement was not repeated on other types of stock.

Collector shoe gear of a new design incorporating a retractable feature operated by a capstan-type hand wheel was fitted to both types of car. This shoe gear was originally mounted on the truck frame independent of the axle boxes, and had to incorporate a compensating bracket to allow for changes in wheel diameter. This shoe gear was unsatisfactory in operation and after a number of years was modified to accept a shoebeam for the positive gear, but still retaining the retractable feature which used a modified hand wheel device placed on the side of the truck frame to lift the negative shoe.

Two successful innovations were introduced on the 'R' stock. One was the provision of tilting mercury-type door interlocks instead of direct contact switches. A

[142]

131 *R47 car*

successful trial of this type of switch had been carried out on the 'F' stock previously, so that it was decided to incorporate this in all future air-door arrangements. The other was a door indicator light fitted on each side of each car, which was illuminated whenever any door interlock contact on that car was not 'made', indicating that a passenger door was 'open'. In this way the guard and platform staff could quickly detect the car which was causing the failure of the guard's pilot light and bell circuit, and so minimize train delays. This feature has been incorporated in all new Tube and Surface rolling stock.

The first batch of 'R' stock cars to replace the hand-worked door stock on the District Line comprised 225 vehicles—143 new cars and 82 converted cars—sufficient to make up 31 trains of both 6- and 8-car formations. The new cars were designated 'R47', although they did not enter service until 1949, and the converted 'Q' trailers were known as 'R38/1' cars. Fifty-four of the new cars were built by Gloucester and 89 by the Birmingham Railway Carriage & Wagon Co.

It was at first considered desirable to convert a block of numbers of 'Q' stock cars, but subsequently it was decided to send cars of the correct type which were due or nearly due for overhaul. The cars scheduled for conversion, therefore, have no relationship to the numbering sequence except that from 013xxx they were converted into No. 1 cars only and from 014xxx were converted into No. 6 cars only. A greater number of 014xxx-numbered cars was converted, because more No. 6 cars than No. 1 cars were required.

In the second stage of the programme, to allow the Circle stock to be replaced, a further 17 trains consisting of 133 cars were required of which 90 were new cars. All but six were non-driving motor cars, and were designated 'R49'—the converted 'Q' trailers were designated 'R38/2'.

At the time the 'R49' cars were ordered it was decided that the underframes and bodies of the new cars should be constructed of aluminium alloy of a corrosion-resistant type. These cars were built by Metropolitan-Cammell. A light alloy was used to reduce the car weight. The weight of a fully-equipped car was, in fact, reduced by 5·4 tons to 28·4 tons by the use of this material. The first light alloy vehicles went into service in May 1952. One car (No. 23567, a No. 5 position car), was left unpainted for a special test. All the other cars were painted in the standard red livery. This single vehicle ran some months in service to ensure that none of the adverse cleaning difficulties which at the time were predicted arose. It was then decided to form a complete unpainted 8-car train, using three of the six new driving motors to provide the driving positions as all other driving motors of 'R' stock were steel cars converted from 'Q' stock trailers.

The 8-car train with unpainted exterior, finished in bright aluminium alloy and a red waistband which was subsequently removed, went into passenger service on 19 January 1953. This train was kept as a block train formation for a number of years until sufficient experience had been gained to justify the subsequent purchase of all new rolling stock externally finished in unpainted light alloy.

Because the 'R' stock trains were virtually formed into block trains, automatic couplers were only provided at the uncoupling positions, so that cars Nos. 4, 5, and 6 had this equipment at one end only. The car at the No. 1 position was not fitted with an automatic coupler, only a Ward type, for use in an emergency only. A Ward to Wedglock adaptor was carried to enable this car to couple to another 'R' stock or an 'O/P' stock train in emergency. Coupling with a 'Q' stock which had the Ward coupling on every car could be made directly.

In 1959, in order to release 'Q' trailers to increase the Circle trains from 5- to 6-cars, it was necessary to provide 1 × 8-car and 2 × 6-car additional trains, so the fleet of 'R' stock was enlarged by 20 cars, 13 being new and 7 being further conversions. These conversions, designated 'R38/3', were carried out this time at Acton Works and not by carbuilders. The new cars were of unpainted light alloy and were designated 'R59', and the converted steel cars were now painted in aluminium to run with the new cars. At the same time a No. 6 'R38' car (No. 22663) was painted aluminium to run with the original unpainted car No. 23567 to make a 'silver' east-end pair.

After the delivery of the 'R59' cars, mixed aluminium and red cars would appear in many trains due to the uncoupling procedures, and it was decided as the 'R' [143]

132 *R49 car*

stock cars passed through Acton Works for overhaul all the stock would be painted aluminium. This decision was taken to assist staff to distinguish easily between 'R' stock and 'CO/CP' stock cars which had a similar physical appearance. The painting of all 'R38/47' stock in aluminium was not completed until 1968.

Another distinctive feature of the 'R' stock was the re-introduction of the use of a roller destination blind instead of enamelled plates. This blind was placed high up near the roof line and not just above the marker-light cabinet.

The 'R' stock was provided with the well-tried PCM type traction control equipment, one equipment controlling two traction motors of type LT111. These motors of 110 h.p. were manufactured by three different manufacturers, G.E.C., Crompton Parkinson, and Metro-Vickers, and incorporated a pressure fan, a new feature which was fitted to the motor on the leading bogie of the driving motor cars. The fan operated a fluid-type speedometer in the driver's cab. While this arrangement was ingenious and fairly robust it had the weakness of being difficult to calibrate accurately, and it was not easy to read at the lower speeds when the driver required help for safe working.

In order to provide some experience with an alternative equipment to the PCM, the seven 'R38/3' cars were fitted with a GEC camshaft equipment which was designed to run in multiple with the PCM. These equipments did not achieve the standard of reliability of the PCM and when some spare PCM equipments became available these cars were converted to PCM. The last car of this type was converted at Acton Works during 1969.

Unfortunately the 'R' stock numbering scheme had been intended to be helpful and simplify recording because the trains operated in block formation. The conversion and delivery programme was too complicated to enable car numbers to give the guide for entry into service. 21xxx cars were west-end driving motor cars and 22xxx were east-end driving motor cars, while 23xxx cars were non-driving motor cars. As each 'R' stock car took up a specific position in a train the middle number or third digit indicated this.

A 6-car train would then read from west to east:

$$211xx-232xx-233xx-234xx+235xx-226xx$$
$$1 \quad - \quad 2 \quad - \quad 3 \quad - \quad 4 \quad + \quad 5 \quad - \quad 6$$

and it was hoped that the last two digits of the 1 to 4 cars would have been the same and similarly the last two digits of the 5 and 6 cars. Once this alignment was broken down it was not possible to correct and very few formations of 4 or 2 cars are working with the numbers in proper sequence. The experience with this train formation encouraged the view that future rolling stock should be formed into interchangeable train units with a simpler numbering arrangement.

34 | 'A' for Amersham Stock

The New Works programme of development for the Metropolitan Line, formulated in 1935, included, in addition to the projection of the Bakerloo Line over the Metropolitan tracks to Stanmore, the four-tracking of the Metropolitan from Harrow to Rickmansworth and the extension of the electrification to Amersham.

Originally it was intended to provide the additional electric stock at that time by conversion of further 'Dreadnought' steam stock to 'T' stock. The outbreak of the Second World War prevented progress being made

with this scheme and all work was subsequently stopped. After the war the financial situation did not allow the scheme to be restarted immediately, but it was evident that the pre-war plans for the rolling stock arrangements had to be recast and that new rolling stock would be required.

The rolling stock designers were then presented with a difficulty because compartment stock with swing doors and a large number of seats had to be replaced by saloon cars with air-doors, fewer seats, and more standing accommodation. The difficulty of operating swing door stock on the 'in town' section of the railway, in addition to the need to provide a through gangway in emergency from car to car for safety reasons in tunnel working, precluded the continuation of the traditional compartment type of rolling stock.

Several designs were considered after the war, and two experimental bodies of the saloon type were built at

133 *Interior 'A' stock*

Acton Works on the underframes of two 'T' stock motor cars which had been withdrawn from service. The first of these two vehicles was numbered 17000, and incorporated a novel seating arrangement which provided a total of 57 seats against the normal 40 for an open saloon car. The layout of the car provided for a through corridor yet divided the car into three sections, each almost self contained except for the corridor provided down one side. Although this corridor was placed down one side, the end doors were fitted in the conventional position on the centre line of the car on top of the central buffers. One serious disadvantage of this layout causing its unpopularity was the fact that it provided hardly any 'window' seats, as most of the seats were installed on 'islands' in the middle of the sections, not against the carbody sides.

The three pairs of double doors fitted down each side

of the car were air-operated and incorporated a novel feature associated with the passenger open control. Both leaves of all doors could be opened and closed by the guard, but each pair of doors was provided with passenger buttons for opening and closing. The opening button only opened one leaf of the pair, while the passenger after entry could reclose this door by pressing a close button also provided. This feature was to try to overcome the objection to air-door stock at exposed terminal stations.

Car 17000 went into passenger service for an experimental period on 26 January 1946. It was subsequently withdrawn for an alteration to the layout and re-entered service again on 2 November 1949, renumbered 17001. A second car numbered 20000 entered service in June 1947, and both ran together coupled to a 'T' stock control trailer No. 6727 which had been modified to

134 *Exterior 'A' stock*

contain door operating gear and lighting switches in the control compartment.

Car 20000 seated 56 passengers all in pairs with a centre gangway, the seats had recessed armrests and moulded back squabs. Although this car also was said to be divided into three sections, it was virtually an open saloon car with two large vestibules placed away from the car ends. The air-door equipment was similar to that provided in car 17000.

In order to test another matter about which there was, and still is, some controversy, one vestibule was provided with doors having a centre pillar dividing the doorway into two sections. This vestibule was also fitted with a vertical handpole in the centre of the floor area. In the other vestibule no centre door pillar was installed, nor was there a centre grab pole in the middle of the circulating area but handgrips were suspended from the car roof.

The two cars were equipped with fluorescent lighting which had at this time not yet been adopted as a standard arrangement for the rolling stock. The motor-alternator providing a.c. power at a frequency of 1200 cycles for both cars was placed on car 17000. Both cars were

135 BELOW—*Driving cab 'A' stock*   **136** RIGHT—*Front view 'A' stock*

carried on 'K2' bogies which were fitted with the standard 36-inch diameter trailer wheels: consideration was given to using British Railways 43½-inch diameter wheels to provide a better riding characteristic, but this idea was never developed.

These cars were finally withdrawn from service in 1953 because the 'T' stock train in which they operated required a second guard to manipulate the door controls, and this was expensive in manpower. The cars were scrapped in 1955, having served their purpose in proving certain arrangements to be incorporated in future rolling stock.

When the programme for replacement of the Metropolitan rolling stock was finally formulated there were five types of rolling stock operating the services from Baker Street, each incompatible with the others. Although one type could sometimes be substituted for another on

some services, this was not always an easy procedure. The 'P' and 'F' stock operated the Uxbridge services with a few 'P' stock journeys occasionally to Watford. The Circle service was operated by 'CP' stock which was 'P' stock converted to PCM control, and these trains worked some of the early main line duties out of Neasden Depot before taking up Circle workings, because at this time this stock was maintained from this depot. The 'T' stock made up into 6- and 8-car formations worked the Watford and Rickmansworth services, while the locomotive-hauled steam stock worked the Aylesbury, Amersham, and Chesham through trains.

In 1959 an order was placed with Cravens of Sheffield for 248 cars to replace the 'T' stock and the locomotive-hauled steam stock, following the extension of the electrified territory from Rickmansworth to Amersham including the branch to Chesham. The letter 'A' was chosen as the alphabet had nearly been exhausted, and 'A' was appropriate for the destination Amersham.

137 *Car 17000. One of the experimental cars that were used to gain information for the 'A' stock production*

Subsequently a further order was placed for 216 similar cars to enable the services to Uxbridge to be provided by the same stock, allowing the 'F' stock to be scrapped and the 'OP' stock to be transferred to the District Line after conversion to PCM control.

The first batch of stock making up 31 × 8-car trains was known as 'A60', while the second batch making up a further 27 × 8-car trains was designated 'A62'. The two batches of stock were virtually identical and interchangeable, being formed into 4-car units—two being coupled together to make an 8-car train. Each unit consisted of two trailer cars between two driving motor cars. The units were not 'handed' and the Wedglock automatic couplers fitted to the outer ends of driving motor cars were provided for 'reversibility'. This avoided the problem which arises with 'non-reversible' stock when a unit turned end for end is unable to couple to a unit which has not been similarly turned. This provision was necessary because of the operation round the Watford triangle layout. The provision of 'reversibility' is obtained by the duplication of train wires through the automatic coupler. Each side of the centre line of the coupler requires to have an identical circuit to the other, and this provision now required 64 connecting studs against 28 only on the 'P' stock. Where the units are non-reversible, the provision of duplicate studs does, of course, improve the circuit reliability, but is only worth doing for this reason where circuit resistance is particularly critical.

The driving motor cars were fitted with 54 seats and the trailer cars with 58. The motor cars had four tip-up seats attached to the bulkhead of the guard's gangway, which was provided in the traditional position at the trailing end of these cars. There was also a seat for the use of the guard placed in the end draughtscreen. All fixed seats were arranged across the cars for three passengers on one side of the gangway and for two on the other side. The rows of seats were arranged to face each other. At the trailer car ends there were two pairs of seats, one each side of the communicating door.

The bodies were constructed mainly of light alloy, but the headstock and bolster underframes were of welded steel fabrication. Light alloy castings were used for doorway and corner pillars, which also formed part of the exterior finish of the cars. Except where these constructional members formed part of the external appearance, the external panelling was of alloy sheet unpainted. The driving cab was fitted with hinged doors, and the guard's gangway had a single air-operated sliding door on each side which could be used by passengers when not occupied by the guard. Two pairs of sliding doors were provided down each side, while the trailer cars had no end doors but three pairs of air-operated doors down each side.

Glass fibre windscreens glazed above the seat backs were installed at all door openings. These screens virtually formed a partition, which carried at roof level across the car a plastic route diagram.

The saloon was illuminated by 4 ft. fluorescent tubes, with 17 in each motor car and one more in trailer cars. These tubes were powered by a.c. supplied from a motor-alternator-rectifier set, the output from the alternator being at 220 volts, 850 cycles. The fluorescent lighting supply was obtained by means of a transformer to bring the voltage down to 115, the frequency remaining at 850. The transformer also fed a germanium full-wave bridge rectifier to provide 50 volts d.c. for the battery supplying the various control circuits. This d.c. voltage was controlled by a magnetic amplifier-type regulator which had no moving parts. The use of this equipment reduced the maintenance liability of the vibrating carbon-type equipment previously installed in earlier types of stock.

The emergency lighting was originally provided by three of the fluorescent lamps fed from the 50-volt d.c. battery supply by individual transistor invertors. This equipment did not prove reliable in service and the cars were later fitted with tungsten emergency lamps fed directly from the battery.

Because of the longer travelling time for passengers on the Metropolitan services the heating installed in the cars was increased from 4 kw. a saloon to 7 kw. a saloon, and this was provided by new-type pyro-bar heaters. All axles of the motor cars were motored so that each motor bogie carried two traction motors of type LT114, manu-

factured by the General Electric Co. These axle-hung motors were of 300 volts, two in permanent series across the line. One PCM traction control unit controlled four motors. Each motor was bolted to a roller suspension sleeve fitted to the axle.

The four-motor traction control equipment was basically similar to the two-motor equipment but designed to withstand a higher current rating. One additional piece of equipment not previously installed was a wheel spin relay to safeguard against one motor of a pair in permanent series spinning.

The differential voltage relay provided had two coils, one across each motor. When the voltage balance between the two becomes disturbed, the line breakers trip out, causing the PCM equipment to return auto-

138 '*A*' *stock motor bogie*

matically to the off position, and the accelerating sequence to restart.

The required train performance necessitated the provision of two accelerating rates and two balancing speeds. A flag switch indicator was installed to control not only the motor field strength but the accelerating rate. With the flag switch down, for operating in the inner section, the master controller would give both accelerating rates, but only full-field strength on the motors would be provided, and consequently a low balancing speed. With the flag switch raised only the low accelerating rate could be used, but the balancing speed would be increased by the selection of 60% field strength for the motors. This field strength provided a maximum speed of 60 m.p.h. for the outer suburban sections.

The car bodies of the 'A' stock were built to the maximum width and length permitted by the Metropolitan loading gauge in order to allow the five seats, plus a gangway, across the car. The width of the cars was 9 ft. 8 in. and the length 53 ft. Considerable criticism of the design of the stock arose because even these dimensions would only provide an 8-car train seating capacity of 464 against 600 with five a side on 'T' stock having the old-fashioned compartments with swing doors. The 'A'

stock train, however, had reasonable standing accommodation for 1,380 passengers; only 900 could be carried on a 'T' stock with five standing in every compartment in great discomfort. The wide vestibules with the air-operated doors gave reasonable standing accommodation for the short-distance passengers, while the transverse seating provided good seating for the long-distance passengers. The design, therefore, gave as much as possible to each of the conflicting requirements of the two types of service the trains had to provide.

The civil engineering works, including the four-tracking to Watford south junction, were completed at the same time as the 'A' stock was introduced, and enabled time-table improvements to be arranged on the Metropolitan Line which, together with the improved reliability of the rolling stock, provided a service never previously achieved.

The electric train service to Chesham with some trains to Amersham began on 12 September 1960, but the 'Steam' stock workings did not cease until almost exactly a year later, when the locomotive change at Rickmansworth was discontinued and London Transport trains ceased to operate beyond Amersham. Soon afterwards most of the Metropolitan services north of Harrow were being provided by 'A' stock trains.

35 | 'C' for Circle Stock

In May 1968 an order was placed with Metropolitan-Cammell Ltd. of Birmingham for a total of 212 cars to make up 35×6-car trains plus two spare cars. Arising out of the integration of the Circle and Hammersmith & City stock, which was achieved when the 'O/P' stock was all converted to PCM equipment and the Circle service raised from 5-car to 6-car formation, it had now become [152] possible to order one set of new stock to continue this integrated policy with economical provision of spare rolling stock. The 35×6-car trains will be required to meet a daily service of 31 trains, 17 for the Hammersmith & City service and 14 for the Circle. This reduction of spares provision has been made possible by the train formation adopted which had to meet two requirements, the operation of 6-car trains in the immediate future and the possibility of an 8-car formation subsequently. After considerable examination of the problems involved, both technical and financial, a 2-car unit was adopted with a driving cab at one end only with the unit fully reversible and all units identical, without having specific 'A' or 'D' ends. The 6-car formations are formed either:

$$M–T \times T–M \times T–M$$
$$\text{or} \quad M–T \times M–T \times T–M$$

The motor car is a driving car with the cab at the outer

139 *C69 Stock/Front view*

end only, and the trailer car has no driving position provided. In normal circumstances an equal number of units will face each way, but in order to equate wheel wear, which in practice has been found to be uneven due to the stock on these lines always working the same way, arrangements are being made in the proposed new timetables to reverse the trains. This can be done easily by working certain Circle train duty cycles to and from the depot by way of Whitechapel.

The new stock has been designated 'C69' stock in the hope that its year of birth would be 1969. In the event this proved to be optimistic and the first trial run of a 4-car train of this stock took place in the summer of 1970. The appearance of the stock is not unlike the 'A' stock in general shape and dimensions, and is of unpainted aluminium alloy construction. While the view of the driving end is very similar to the 'A' stock, the side elevation appearance and dimensions are different.

Some difference in dimensions is produced by the fact that the general arrangement drawings of this stock have been set out in metric units for the first time. The 'A' stock cars, both motor and trailer, were 53 ft. 0½ in. over body ends; the driving motor car of 'C69' is 52 ft. 7 in. (16,030 mm.) and the trailer car 49 ft. (14,940 mm.). The difference between the two types of car has been brought about by arranging for the passenger accommodation in both cars to be the same and adding to the driving motor car one driving cab. In order to reduce the body overhang by this arrangement the bogie centres of the two cars are different. The driving motor car has bogie centres 35 ft. 6 in. (10,820 mm.), which is the same as 'A' stock but the trailer car has bogie centres of 31 ft. 6 in. (9,600 mm.).

Each car is provided with four pairs of double doors down each side to give the maximum passenger flow on the Circle service, where passengers only travel for short distances and there is a constant interchange. Between each pair of double doors pairs of facing seats are fitted, while at the body ends including the cab-end of the motor car, longitudinal seats for two on each side are provided. These arrangements have reduced the number of seats available in each car to 32. The 'A' stock had 54 seats in the motor cars and 58 in the trailer cars. A great deal of additional circulating and standing space has been arranged which, together with the setting back of the windscreens so that doorways are not obstructed by standing passengers, will ensure the reduction of station stop times at critical stations.

A 6-car train will have a length of 93 metres (309 ft. 8½ in. over buffers), which is controlled at present by the [153]

140 *C69 Stock/Interior view*

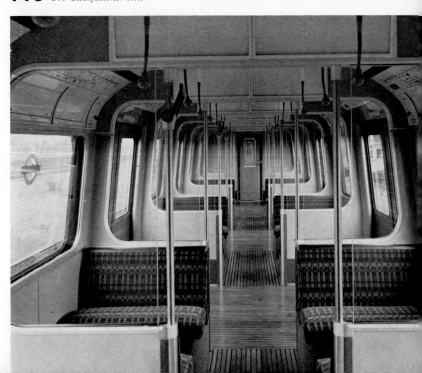

limitation imposed by Circle Line stations between High Street Kensington and Paddington, and the stations on the Hammersmith & City Line. This length has also been influenced by the fact that provision has been made for this stock to be operated by one man when it is essential that the leading driving cab should be at the station platform.

The ventilation of the car body is provided by fixed openings above cant rail level, similar to the arrangement

[154]

141 *C69 Stock/Combined motor-controller handle and console*

installed on the 1967 Tube stock on the Victoria Line and not by hinged ventilators of the design incorporated in 'A' stock, but in addition roof-mounted heater/blower equipment is being used for the first time in general service on Underground rolling stock.

The air-operated sliding doors are top-hung with an open-type sill plate to reduce the problems associated with door obstruction interfering with the proper closing of the doors. With one-man operation it is necessary to ensure that the doors are closed before the train can be permitted to start, and not just do away with the guard's starting signal. Door indicator lights showing the car where the doors are not properly closed are installed.

The door-control equipment has been fitted in the driving cab and not in the conventional position at the trailing-end gangway. This arrangement is to facilitate one-man operation, although the equipment is so arranged that the door control can be worked from any cab on the train. An additional facility has been arranged to avoid the necessity for all the doors to remain open at terminal stations. A selective 'close' button has been fitted which will close three of the four pairs of double doors.

One of the most novel features of this stock is the introduction of an air-operated sliding door to the driver's cab, with draughtproofing provided by blow-up air seals. This air seal is fed by an air valve operated by the movement of the door engine arm. Provision has also been made for this door to be opened by a key from the outside or by staff from the inside in depots when air is not available. The cab doors are interlocked at the driver's end with the traction control circuit to ensure that the train does not move off with these doors open.

The auxiliary power supply is obtained from a motor-alternator-rectifier unit carried on the motor car of the AEI MG 3007 AY type, which produces a.c. at 230 volts,

850 cycles a second. The output from this machine is then treated in several ways for auxiliary purposes. A transformer converts the 230-volt supply to 115 volts without alteration of the frequency for the main fluorescent lighting circuits. A rectifier unit converts the a.c. supply to 50 volt d.c. for charging the auxiliary battery and providing control current. This 50-volt d.c. supply is re-inverted to produce 230 volts, 50 cycles a second a.c. for the provision of power to the blower/heater fans and for the emergency lights.

The main lighting is supplied chiefly by 4 ft. (there are some 2 ft.) fluorescent tubes powered from the 850-cycle supply. Emergency lighting if the motor alternator shuts down is obtained by supplying two tubes in each car from the 50-volt d.c. battery through an inverter.

The four blower/heater units are fitted in the ceiling of each car, each capable of providing 1·8 kw. of heat.

The inverter carried on the trailer car supplies the four fans on the driving motor car as well as those on the trailer car. The fans can deliver hot or cold air according to whether heating or ventilation is required. A thermostat is provided to control the heating. In addition to the saloon heating a blower/heater is installed in the cab which is under the driver's control.

Also carried on the trailer car is a compressor, either a Reavell/Mawdsley two-cylinder type TBC38Z or a Westinghouse three-cylinder type 3HC43 machine; an equal number of each has been provided. Compressor synchronization which ensures that all compressors

RIGHT—*C69 Stock/Looking towards one of the door control panels*

normally operate on a train when replenishing the air supply is provided by a new method. Each compressor contactor has two operating coils, one fed from each end of the train, which provides greater reliability by dupli-

143 *C69 Stock/Half open side door of cab*

cating the control feeds.

The 2-car units have automatic couplers at the outer ends, and because of the reversibility feature and the provision of additional equipment controls, a total of 76 studs have now to be provided against the 64 required by the 'A' stock reversible units. Space for the additional studs has been found by reducing their diameter in all but the centre row, which have been arranged to carry those circuits with the heavier currents.

Various features introduced in the 1967 Tube stock have been incorporated. The control feature, which enables the driver to isolate from his leading cab part of the train, has been provided. However, because the train formation is six cars composed of 3 × 2-car units the train cannot be conveniently halved as in the 1967 Tube stock. On the 'C69' stock this has necessitated the provision of some of the additional control wires across the automatic couplers.

Provision has also been made for similar communication systems to those provided on the 1967 Tube stock, but initially the inter-train radio and the carrier wave system will not be provided as this equipment cannot be used until all trains using the tracks are similarly equipped. In the first place, therefore, only a public address system has been fitted which will enable the driver to address the passengers and a cab-to-cab telephone enabling speech between all driving cabs to be arranged.

The driving motor cars have four traction motors of type LT117, manufactured by Brush of Loughborough, mounted on Timken roller suspension sleeves in a similar manner to 'A' stock. The motors, however, are of a design giving a higher speed, running at 3,800 r.p.m. at a train speed of 60 m.p.h., with a gear ratio of 94/14 and 36-inch diameter motor wheels. This speed will not be achieved on the Circle or Hammersmith & City operations, however. The small pinion size required for this gear ratio has necessitated the provision of a 'plug-in' pinion for the first time. This means that the pinion is made integral with a small shaft which is pressed into the end of the armature shaft. All pinions on previous stocks have been shrunk on to the armature shaft. The motor, too, has a circular frame instead of the 'octagonal' traditional type traction motor frame.

The motors for 'C69' stock are of the 300-volt type, two being arranged in permanent series. The control is provided by PCM-type equipment manufactured by A.E.I. Ltd., but arranged to give rheostatic braking by the system first introduced on the Victoria Line on the 1967 Tube stock. The 'C69' stock, however, being marginally heavier with higher speeds having to be catered for, the equipment is modified accordingly. In addition there are two new features of this equipment; the provision of virtually constant acceleration irrespective of train loading conditions and the external excitation of the motors to ensure the build up of rheostatic braking which has already been mentioned.

The bogies are provided with chevron rubber type axle-boxes, but the secondary suspension between the body and the bogies incorporates the use of air-metacone suspension. This rubber/air springing unit is so arranged that in the unloaded condition as the weight of the body increases by the acceptance of passengers, air is admitted to the metacone unit carried on either side of the bogie which automatically maintains the car height. This feature of the car springing is used to control both the acceleration and the braking since it is equivalent to weighing the passenger load on the car. The air suspension pressure, therefore, has a control effect on the rate coil setting of the notching relay of the PCM control equipment, and thereby ensures sensibly constant acceleration irrespective of load. A variable load valve controlled by the air pressure setting from this suspension arrangement also controls the maximum brake pressure applied to the car. Braking forces up to the point of wheel pick-up for each car can, therefore, be arranged, and not limited by the braking rate which may pick up the wheels on the least loaded car. Higher accelerating and braking rates can safely be arranged on trains having this equipment. The resetting of the air-metacone suspension is arranged to take place each time the doors are opened.

The braking arrangement for this stock provides for [157]

144 *C69 Stock/Bogie mounted*

the minimum rate to be achieved on the driving motor cars by rheostatic braking applied, which will then be supplemented as required by air-brakes on the trailers, followed by air-brakes on the driving motor cars. The effective overall braking rate required at any time, and whichever combination of air and dynamic braking is needed to effect it, is controlled by a series of mercury retardation controllers.

A handbrake or parking brake is provided in each driver's cab which is hydraulically actuated. To assist the driver and reduce the physical effort needed in applying this brake a motor-driven pump is fitted to provide the hydraulic pressure, but it is possible to apply the brake without the assistance of this device by means of an emergency hand-pump.

The trains are not provided with ATO (Automatic Train Operation) but provision has been made for such equipment. This feature, like the higher performance through increased acceleration and braking, will not be fully utilized on Circle workings until all the older cars with which they will initially inter-run have been replaced.

The introduction of the 'C69' stock enables the 'Q' stock on the District to be replaced by 'CO/CP' stock from Hammersmith. The District Line workings will then all be provided by two types of rolling stock, the 'R' or 'CO/CP' stock. This arrangement will continue until 1977/78, when 'CO/CP' stock falls due for replacement and it will then be necessary to decide whether a further batch of 'C' stock is purchased or a new brand of car type 'D' for District will appear.

A note on the carbuilders and principal equipment contractors

Throughout these pages many firms that have been associated with the building of the Metropolitan and District Line rolling stock have been mentioned. Some of these names have now disappeared, having been absorbed, amalgamated, or ceased to trade, but they are linked with the development of London's Underground and a brief historical review is not out of place.

The largest portion of the rolling stock of London's Underground has been built by Metro Cammell Ltd. of Birmingham or its predecessors. This company originated from the railway rolling stock manufacturing business set up at Saltley in 1835, then a village on the outskirts of Birmingham, by Joseph Wright, a London coachbuilder. This business was conducted under the title of Joseph Wright & Sons until 1862, when it became the Metropolitan Railway Carriage & Wagon Co. Ltd.

In 1902 the Metropolitan Amalgamated Railway Carriage & Wagon Co. Ltd. was formed by the combination of this concern with four other carbuilders:

(1) The Ashbury Railway Carriage & Iron Co. Ltd. with works at Openshaw, Manchester;

(2) Brown Marshalls & Co. Ltd. with works at Adderley Park, Birmingham;

(3) The Lancaster Railway Carriage & Wagon Co. Ltd. with works in Lancaster;

(4) The Oldbury Railway Carriage & Wagon Co. Ltd., Oldbury, Birmingham.

Following a number of other financial exchanges, including the acquisition of a substantial interest in Docker Bros., the paint manufacturers, the name of the concern was changed in 1912 to the Metropolitan Carriage, Wagon & Finance Co. Ltd.

In 1917 this company, in conjunction with Vickers Ltd., the steel and shipbuilding concern, acquired a controlling interest in the British Westinghouse Electric & Manufacturing Co. Ltd. which in 1919 changed its name to Metropolitan Vickers Electrical Co. Ltd. At this time, too, an exchange of shares was arranged so that the Metropolitan Carriage, Wagon & Finance Company became a wholly-owned subsidiary of Vickers Ltd.

Ten years later in 1929, Vickers and Cammell Laird (both in the steel and shipbuilding industry) decided to amalgamate their carbuilding interests, forming the Metropolitan-Cammell Carriage, Wagon & Finance Co. Ltd. to control these interests. This re-organization gave the carbuilding concern a controlling interest in the Midland Railway Carriage & Wagon Co. Ltd., with further premises in the Birmingham area, and in the Leeds Forge Co. Ltd. As a result, the Metropolitan-Cammell railway rolling stock manufacturing became concentrated in three large factories, located at Saltley and Washwood Heath in Birmingham and at Old Park in Wednesbury. All these works shared in the manufacture of rolling stock for London Transport or its predecessors.

In 1934 the 'Finance' part of the name of the company was dropped and in a further reorganization in 1965 the company became Metropolitan-Cammell Ltd. The carbuilding activities were then confined to Washwood Heath. The 'C69' stock is the latest product from these works.

Cravens of Sheffield were also carbuilders of long standing but, apart from some steam stock for the Metropolitan Railway, had never built electric multiple unit stock until the order for the 'A' stock was placed with the Company in 1958. In 1965 Cravens transferred their carbuilding business to Metropolitan-Cammells.

The Brush Electrical Engineering Co. Ltd., of Loughborough, has built few cars for London Transport fleet after being concerned with the construction of the original District Railway electric rolling stock, although in the citation of incorporation dating from 1889 it was described as manufacturer of all kinds of electrical plant and machinery, railway and tramway rolling stock, and body work for public utility vehicles. After many years with little interest in London's Underground, it is now concerned with the manufacture of the traction motors for the 'C69' stock by the merging of its traction interests with Crompton Parkinson Ltd. of Chelmsford.

This latter firm has slightly deeper roots, being registered in 1888 as Crompton & Co. Ltd., and being concerned with the early electric traction equipment for the City & South London Railway. The name was changed in 1927 to Crompton Parkinson Ltd. after amalgamation with E. & A. Parkinson Ltd. In 1966 the business was acquired by the Hawker Siddeley Group which had already obtained control of Brush and the traction interests have now been merged with those of Brush.

Another carbuilding firm which has built a number of cars for London Transport in the past is the Gloucester Railway Carriage & Wagon Co. Ltd., originally registered in 1860 as the Gloucester Wagon Co. Ltd. This concern is now a member of the Babcock & Wilcox Group and specializes in bogie manufacture, but has not participated in London Transport requirements since the 'R' stock.

[160] So far, no personal names of the many people involved in these companies' activities have been mentioned. Although they are legion, just the industrial essentials are necessary to these notes, but one name must be mentioned, that of George Westinghouse—a veritable giant of a man in the industrial field. George Westinghouse was born as long ago as 1846, and not only invented the air-brake which will forever carry his name, but also developed a vast electrical industry. In 1889 the Westinghouse Electric Co. of London was formed, which, after the acquisition of land at Trafford Park, Manchester, became in 1899 the British Westinghouse Electric & Manufacturing Co. Ltd. The main purpose behind the establishment of this concern on the scale which it was initially planned was to provide a means of electrifying the railways of Great Britain! All the technical 'know how' was initially to be provided by the parent American firm, the Westinghouse Electric Company of Pittsburgh. An American financial crisis and the First World War did not help the finances of the British Westinghouse concern, and in 1919 (as has already been mentioned) the name was changed to Metropolitan-Vickers Electrical Co. Ltd. following its acquisition by the Vickers group from the American Westinghouse interests.

In 1928 the Vickers Group sold its interest in Metropolitan-Vickers to the International General Electric Company of the United States, which already controlled the British Thomson-Houston Co. Ltd., and this set the stage for the formation of Associated Electrical Industries Ltd. as the holding company for both concerns which continued to trade as separate organizations until 1967. The International General Electric Company in 1952 relinquished management control, but the interchange of technical information and patent rights was maintained for many years, and this enabled the PCM type of traction control equipment to be developed specially by the BTH company for service on London's Underground from basic designs provided by the American General Electric Company.

The British-Thomson-Houston Co. Ltd. was, in fact, formed in 1896 to exploit in the United Kingdom and Europe the patents of the American Thomson Houston Company which, following amalgamations in America, became the General Electric Company of America. The name of the English associate could not be changed to General Electric Company because such a concern, purely of English origin, had already existed since 1889.

The recent amalgamation of A.E.I., G.E.C., and English Electric interests has brought all the electric traction matters of these concerns under the control of A.E.I.-English Electric Traction Ltd., and the 'C69' stock PCM traction equipment has now been manufactured by this concern.

The traction motors originally manufactured by BTH always bore the prefix letters GE following the American designs of this associated concern. The (British) General Electric Company when it began manufacturing traction motors, therefore, used the letters WT (after Witton, where the works were situated).

The Westinghouse-designed motors were not officially distinguished by the use of a letter but a W was often used for convenience. Later, when the name was changed, MV was used. In 1938 a motor was designed by Crompton Parkinson to London Transport requirements to be constructed by any traction motor builder, and the LT.100 came into being which was, in fact, manufactured both by the General Electric (British) and Crompton Parkinson.

The LT.111 for the 'R' stock was manufactured by three motor manufacturers—Cromptons, Metro-Vickers, and BTH—and all motors since have been specially designed to London Transport requirements and have, therefore, borne the letters LT instead of those of the manufacturer.

The Underground group of companies tried car-building on its own account by bringing into activity the Union Construction Co., in 1925, to reconstruct the Central London Railway tube cars from hand-manipulated gates to air-operated doors. Having set up the organization for this purpose including premises at Feltham, Middlesex, it was a short step to the building of rolling stock *de novo*. Large numbers of tube cars were built, and tramcars known as 'Felthams' or U.C.C. cars, but in addition a batch of District stock was completed in 1932.

The Union Construction Co. originated in 1901 in the fashion of contemporary American traction business to construct the property of the parent operating concern. If the parent concern was financially unstable the 'Construction' company would lease or lend the operating equipment which it had built until the financial situation improved. In the event the Metropolitan District with which it was associated did not need this support, although it was far from being financially robust, so the Union Construction Co. was not required to function at this time. The opportunity came, however, in 1925, with the heavy programme of modernization of the tube rolling stock subsequently extended to the modernization of the associated tramcar fleets.

To accord with the principle of leasing and lending of equipment the name of the company was changed on 4 February 1929 to the Union Construction & Finance Co. Ltd.

Under Section 21 of the London Passenger Transport Act of 1933, which created London Transport, the new Board formed at that time was expressly forbidden to manufacture rolling stock except of an experimental nature. The Union Construction & Finance Co. Ltd., therefore, ceased to exist on 1 July 1933.

Another carbuilding name which has ceased to manufacture rolling stock for the Underground is Hurst Nelson & Co. Ltd. of Motherwell, Scotland, which became a public company in 1909 and was very active in the building of tramcars over the golden years of electric tramway construction. Apart from the 'C' stock built in 1911, the company did not maintain its interest in the supply of vehicles to London.

The Westinghouse Brake & Signal Co. Ltd., together with its predecessors, has been responsible for providing the air-brake equipment when fitted for practically all the rolling stock of London's Underground. This concern originated in England in 1881 as the Westinghouse Brake Co. Ltd. to exploit George Westinghouse's brake patents. Subsequently, interest in signalling equipment was acquired, and the combination of these two interests has played no small part in enabling equipment to be manufactured which made the automatic train control system used on the Victoria Line a reality.

A note on electric braking

Because a direct current motor and a direct current generator are basically the same machine it follows that any d.c. motor, if driven by an external power source, will generate electricity. This fundamental fact means that electric braking of a train using direct current traction motors is possible. During motoring, electrical energy is taken from the supply system and converted into movement or kinetic energy as the train accelerates. During electric braking this kinetic energy is converted back into electric energy as the train slows down.

There are two fundamental but related systems of electric braking, sometimes called dynamic braking, using ordinary direct current traction motors (a) rheostatic braking and (b) regenerative braking. In rheostatic braking the electrical energy developed by the motors is fed or loaded on to resistances carried on the train itself, and the energy generated is dissipated in heating up these resistances. In regenerative braking, the energy developed is returned to the supply system for other customers to use, so reducing the load on the power plant and actually saving electrical energy. Since the introduction of electric traction, engineers have tried to find solutions to the problems involved. Unfortunately, as with many other things which are basically simple, there prove to be many complications and difficulties in actual practice.

The first two problems which have to be overcome in electric braking are to absorb the maximum kinetic energy at the start of braking, smoothing it off as this energy is absorbed or lost when the speed comes down;

and secondly to bring the train to rest at the correct point when little kinetic energy is left at the low speed.

As the kinetic energy is proportional to the square of the speed, most of the generation of electricity occurs at the beginning of the braking cycle. For example, if a train is being braked electrically from a speed of 40 m.p.h. there is only one-sixteenth of the total energy left below a speed of 10 m.p.h. Provision, therefore, is made in most systems for a friction brake to take over to stop the train. The transition from electric brake to friction brake has to be smooth and although the solution to this problem is not simple it can be achieved.

When a rheostatic system is employed it has the advantage of being independent of the power supply and track conditions, and the controls applied are consistent for each and every braking stop.

The spreading of the electricity load throughout the braking cycle with a rheostatic system is relatively simple in that it is the opposite of acceleration and can be obtained by limiting the current generated to a pre-determined amount and when this begins to fall off, arrangements are made for the friction brake to take over.

Having realized that it is relatively simple to make motors generate electricity under braking conditions, it follows that this electricity could be available for useful work elsewhere, and such a system would be described as regenerative. However, under a regenerative braking system, it is the voltage which has to be limited because this is controlled by that of the supply system into which the regenerated current must be pumped without a severe limitation on the current being regenerated. Therefore, the size of the motors, power cables and switch gear must

145 *An opened split-frame traction motor similar in mechanical construction to the 50M and 86M types used by the Metropolitan Railway. This machine, however, is of a later type including interpoles not fitted to the original Metropolitan machines (A.E.I.)*

146 *MD53-type metadyne machine from the regulator and exciter end on the ventilating duct side. This machine weighed about 3 tons and was suspended along the centre of the car underframe (A.E.I.)*

be robust enough to withstand overloads under excessive braking conditions. Unfortunately, because electricity can be stored in only relatively small amounts, it must be used immediately it is produced. If electric train braking is to be of value, then the energy changed into electricity must be used elsewhere at once. The greatest problem in this connection, however, is that most of the energy produced from braking occurs in the first phase of the braking.

In simple terms, this means that for every train being stopped three must be starting up at the same time to use the electricity being produced. This situation is virtually impossible so that arrangements must be made for the system to be receptive whether other trains are

starting up or not, by having some artificial load available either at substations or on the trains to absorb the excess energy which cannot be used as it is produced.

The Metropolitan Railway carried out some experiments at Neasden with two electric locomotives obtained from the Central London Railway in 1905 when these were offered for sale following the introduction of multiple unit trains. The system employed for these experiments was one proposed by Raworth which had been successfully applied to tramcars. While it could be said that there was no difficulty in getting generation, there was considerable trouble in controlling it to do just what was required in stopping a train at a fixed point. Making an electric train accelerate from rest is a simple matter and variations in performance from one vehicle to another in the train are not critical. But to stop a train at an accurate final point of rest, taking into account variations in performance between vehicles on the train, becomes difficult.

It is one thing to achieve regeneration on a locomotive in which all the controls and switchings are related to one set of equipment, but with a multiple unit system where several equipments have to work in unison, further complications arise.

The metadyne system introduced to London Transport in 1936 on the 'O' stock was the first multiple unit control system in the world which incorporated a practical regenerative braking system. The term 'metadyne' is derived from the Greek and means 'conversion of power.' The metadyne was a rotating machine interposed between the supply line and the traction motors which, putting it very simply, converted a constant voltage supply to a constant current output.

This is basically what a series-parallel resistance control system tries to do in a very crude way. The constant voltage from the 600-volt supply is reduced by inserting resistance so that the current supplied to the motors is limited to a maximum value. As this current falls with the rotation of the motors so resistance is cut out in a series of notches restoring the current to the maximum value, until full speed is reached. The metadyne did this without using resistances, maintaining a smooth accelerating current without any notching. The main advantage of the system, however, was that in reverse a current at low voltage which determined the braking rate provided by the traction motor was converted to a high voltage which could be pumped back into the supply line to do useful work elsewhere.

When receptive line conditions existed an excellent rate of regeneration was achieved but conditions were not always right and because the substations were not receptive the selection switches carried on the trains more often than not cut the regenerative system out, substituting rheostatic braking. This was not unsatisfactory since electric braking was still available, saving brake blocks and giving a smooth stop. The metadyne system was a technical achievement of considerable merit but unfortunately did not gain the success it deserved mainly for two reasons; the power supply system was not designed to accept a regenerative system and the equipment was complicated and less reliable to a very large degree in general operation than contemporary series-parallel equipments. The equipment was also very heavy.

With the lack of complete success of the metadyne system which would not have been suitable in any case for tube rolling stock because of the limited clearances for the housing of the additional equipment, the development of electric braking on the London Underground was allowed to lapse. The feeling persisted, however, that a potential source of energy was being wasted and that some savings could be achieved if some form of electric braking were produced and, beginning in 1957, experiments were conducted on a further regenerative system. This system was very complex and required the provision of a bus line to tie the multiple unit equipments together to avoid the effect of current rail gaps. The provision of a bus line was considered to be a retrograde step for safety from fusing incidents and the scheme was abandoned.

It was thought, however, that some advantage could be obtained by utilizing the experience gained to develop a rheostatic braking scheme which would not require bus lines and which could be applied to a multiple unit train. Rheostatic braking had already been applied on many systems throughout the world where all the train axles were motored. This is an expensive practice both in capital and maintenance when the acceleration required of the train formations does not warrant this provision.

[165]

147 *MV145AZ traction motor associated with metadyne control—the extra two power leads are to provide the separately excited field windings* (A.E.I.)

However, where only 50% of the axles are motored the problem of apportioning train braking between the motors and the friction brakes can only be solved by complicated equipment which increases the cost.

An equipment for providing rheostatic braking with only 50% axles motored was developed for the Victoria Line stock and has been applied to the new 'C69' stock, now entering service. This type of equipment can only be proved as a financial success after a long service experience. There is no doubt that it is a technical

success. The advantages are a reduction in brake block and wheel wear with a consequent reduction in the accumulation of dust in the tunnels.

The scheme adopted has been built round the well-tried PCM traction control system and, therefore, utilizes the control units which have already proved reliable in service. The rheostatic scheme, however, requires virtually two equipments, where only one was needed for accelerating the train, and in addition it requires complicated equipment to transfer from electric braking to the friction brake.

With a multiple unit train operating a rapid transit type of service, an infinite variety of braking rates is not required because a predictable service pattern can be established. Only three rates of braking are provided: (a) rheostatic on the motored axles only, (b) rheostatic on the motored axles together with friction brake on the trailer axles, and (c) friction brake on all axles. The selection of the rate of braking on the Victoria Line is outside the control of the driver because of the automatic train control and the variation between the three rates of braking is automatically adjusted. On the 'C69' stock the rheostatic brake will be automatically applied when a brake is called for and only if the braking rate is insufficient will the air-brake apply the brake blocks under the control of the mercury retarder.

Unfortunately a rheostatic braking system does nothing towards conserving energy or keeping down the tunnel temperatures, which is the advantage of a full regenerative braking scheme. So engineers must continue to search for a solution to the problems involved in providing a fully regenerative scheme.

Index

Printed in Great Britain by Tapp & Toothill Ltd., Leeds and London

Early Metropolitan Railway device, based on the Company's seal. It includes the arms of the City of London (St. George's Cross with the sword of St. Paul) above a representation of steam-hauled trains in twin single-line tunnels. In fact, the Metropolitan Railway was built in double-line tunnel. The seal, used from 1854 to 1933, showed the trains in reversed positions, in accordance with heraldic convention

Device used by the Metropolitan District Railway (but never on rolling stock) showing shields of the City of London (centre), City of Westminster (right), and pre-1910 County of Middlesex (left). The stylised locomotive bore no relation to any which ran on the District. The specimen illustrated is from a painted glass window formerly in the Company's board room